The Buddha *before* Buddhism

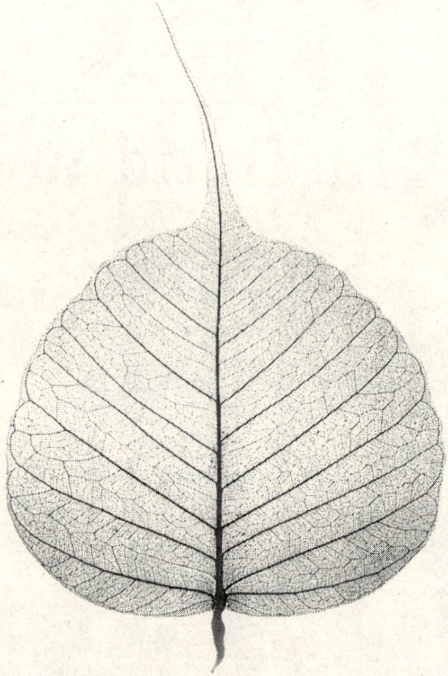

The Buddha *before* Buddhism

WISDOM FROM THE EARLY TEACHINGS

GIL FRONSDAL

JAICO PUBLISHING HOUSE

Ahmedabad Bangalore Chennai
Delhi Hyderabad Kolkata Mumbai

Published by Jaico Publishing House
A-2 Jash Chambers, 7-A Sir Phirozshah Mehta Road
Fort, Mumbai - 400 001
jaicopub@jaicobooks.com
www.jaicobooks.com

Published in arrangement with
Shambhala Publications, Inc.
4720 Walnut Street
#106, Boulder, Colorado 80301, USA
www.shambhala.com

THE BUDDHA BEFORE BUDDHISM
ISBN 978-93-86867-29-2

First Jaico Impression: 2018

Printed by
Trinity Academy For Corporate Training Limited, Mumbai

Contents

Preface

THIS BOOK IS a translation of a collection of ancient Buddhist poems often considered to be among the Buddha's first teachings. The anthology's original title, the *Book of Eights,* suggests something about the format of the poems, but it gives no hint that the text contains a radical message that differs significantly from standard presentations of Buddhism. Nor does the traditional title indicate that the book's teachings offer people a provocative challenge to live a life of deep, abiding peace. The peace that this text holds at its center is one to be experienced here and now, without any reference to the ultimate metaphysical and religious realities often taught as fundamental to Buddhism. In this text, reality is not divided into a conditioned, worldly realm and an unconditioned, transcendent realm far removed from the contingent world of ordinary human life. Instead, the teachings point to a peace that can be found in this life in this world. References to rarefied states of mental attainments—usually associated with meditation adepts

—are also absent from this text, except perhaps in one enigmatic statement (verse 874).

As a longtime Buddhist practitioner, I am inspired by the directness, simplicity, and immediacy of the vision pointed to by these poems. Some Buddhist teachers have suggested that what is presented here is the view of the world as seen by someone who is already enlightened and that the *Book of Eights* represents the perspectives of those furthest along the Buddhist path. Whether this is the case or not, I believe the text teaches a possibility that is available to anyone. I hope this translation helps open up this possibility.

In translating the text, I attempted to understand its teachings as intended by its author(s), trying to be as aware as possible of the biases and modern ideas I naturally carry with me. The purpose for doing this translation work was intensely personal in that I wanted to be challenged by these ancient teachings. I also hoped my own understanding of Buddhist teachings would improve through a closer look at some of its earliest texts.

To arouse interest in a translation of one of the oldest surviving Buddhist texts, I decided to call this book *The Buddha before Buddhism*. I hoped this title would raise a number of questions—most prominently, what might the Buddha have taught after his awakening but before he and others organized and systematized his teachings into what is now identified as Buddhism? Here, in an incipient stage in the development of early Buddhism, can we identify the Buddha's most essential message?

Acknowledgments

IN THE YEARS that I have studied and translated the *Book of Eights,* I have been inspired and supported by many people. I thank David Chappell, who introduced me to this text in my first graduate course in Buddhist studies. Jan Nattier's translation of a few of the discourses from the anthology gave me my first orientation for studying the text in Pali. Jan's ongoing encouragement and guidance throughout the project have been invaluable. I am also grateful to Grace G. Burford for her book *Desire, Death, and Goodness*: *The Conflict of Ultimate Values in Theravada Buddhism.* Her study on the *Book of Eights* inspired me with new perspectives for reading the text.

I am very grateful to Thanissaro Bhikkhu, Andrew Olendzki, and Diana Clark for checking my translation against the Pali original. I thank Bhikkhu Bodhi for his comments on my translation of "The Eightfold Discourse on the Ultimate." The suggestions and corrections from these scholars have been as humbling as they have been invaluable.

Diana Clark and Carol Ghigliari both provided expert editing of the entire book. Without their generous help, the text wouldn't be as readable as it has become. Andrea Fella provided important editorial suggestions on the translation of the poems. I am very grateful for their contributions and their warmhearted support.

I am also grateful to the pioneering scholarship of those who previously translated the text into English. Their careful work at deciphering some of the difficult passages made it possible for me to make my own translation. In particular, I wish to thank K. R. Norman and Thanissaro Bhikkhu.

I would like to reassure all those who have supported me in this project that any errors in the translation are my own.

The Buddha before Buddhism

Introduction

THE *BOOK OF EIGHTS,* or *Aṭṭhakavagga,* is a relatively small anthology of sixteen poems tucked away in a larger anthology that is itself relegated to yet another anthology, the canonical group of texts known as the *Minor Collection* (*Khuddaka Nikāya*). Perhaps because of this inconspicuous placement, the *Book of Eights* has not received the attention it deserves for containing a unique and, for some, a very inspiring presentation of important Buddhist teachings. Here we find the Buddha's teachings pared down to their most essential elements, free of the more complex doctrines often associated with Buddhism. The *Book of Eights* gives the impression of containing the seeds that grew into the fully developed early Buddhist teachings in India.

What may be perplexing to many is that the *Book of Eights* does not espouse a religious doctrine that exists in opposition to other doctrines. Nor does it put forth a teaching that is meant to be seen as superior to other teachings. In a manner that challenges the religious beliefs of many people—including many Buddhists—the text explicitly denies the role of ultimate religious "truth" and "knowledge" in attaining personal peace.

Instead, the text points to a direct and simple approach for attaining peace without requiring an adherence to any specific ideology. The possibility of this peace is what guides the teachings and practices in the text. The value of these teachings is not the profundity of their philosophy or their authority as "scripture"; rather, they are valuable for the results they bring to those who live by them. Instead of doctrines to be believed, the *Book of Eights* describes means or practices for realizing peace.

The goal put forth in the *Book of Eights* is described both in terms of the states of mind to be attained and the mental activities to be abandoned. Peace and equanimity are the most common descriptions of what is attained,[1] and clinging, craving, being entrenched, and quarreling are the activities most frequently said to be abandoned.[2] There is a clear relationship between the states to be attained and the activities to be let go in that to experience peace for oneself, one must release one's clingings. The person who realizes this is called a sage, or *muni*, an ancient Indian designation for a wise or holy person. In much later Buddhist literature, the Buddha is referred to as Sakyamuni—that is, "the Sage of the Sakya [Clan]."

While the attainment of peace is often referred to in personal terms, the *Book of Eights* also places its teaching in the context of social strife. This is seen dramatically in the opening of "The Discourse on Being Violent"

(Chapter 15), where the Buddha recounts his dismay at the quarrels and conflicts he witnessed in his own society. In "The Discourse to Pasūra" (Chapter 8), the Buddha is keenly sensitive to the suffering that comes from doctrinal conflicts between rival religious groups. Many of the poems in the *Book of Eights* emphasize that a sage does not get involved in these interpersonal and interreligious conflicts. Because the book frequently discusses social conflict and the avoidance of such conflict, the teachings not only point to the possibility of personal peace, but they also suggest the possibility of peace between people as well.

Remarkably, the teachings in the *Book of Eights* are presented without recourse to many of the standard, systematized teachings associated with early Buddhism. No mention is made of most of the familiar numbered lists such as the Four Noble Truths and the Eightfold Path—teachings that are often considered to be the essence of Buddhism. Nowhere in the text does one find the Four Foundations of Mindfulness, the four *jhānas* (concentration states), the Five Aggregates, the Three Characteristics, the Seven Factors of Awakening, or the Three Refuges. Also missing are the teachings that modern audiences often find the most confusing, such as the concepts of not-self and an unconditioned reality that transcends ordinary life. The common Buddhist concerns of rebirth and ending the cycles of rebirth are primarily discussed in terms of what non-Buddhists believe. The *Book of Eights'* emphasis is on overcoming any longing for any form of future rebirth. In contrast to later Buddhist teachings that are predicated on the belief in rebirth, the *Book of Eights* presents a path of practice—attainable in this lifetime—that appears free from concern with multiple lives.

The absence of standardized and systematized teachings is one reason the *Book of Eights* is easy to overlook. It doesn't provide numerical lists or easy quotes to illustrate the teachings found in introductory-level books on Buddhism. The text can also be dismissed if one is looking for a devotional-based orientation to Buddhism and the Buddha. In this text, the Buddha does not appear in superhuman forms or with supernatural powers that would inspire devotees. Nowhere is he called "the One Who Is Thus" (*tathāgata*), a title frequently associated with him in other early scriptures. Even the title of Buddha is rare, occurring only once. Furthermore, only once in the verses is he referred to by the illustrious title "the Blessed One" (*bhagavant*).

Because the teachings of the *Book of Eights* differ from what is generally understood to be the Buddha's message, a few scholars have suggested that it was not originally a Buddhist text. These scholars believe that one or more converts from another religious group may have brought the text along when they joined the Buddha's order. Because the text was seen as compatible with early Buddhist teachings, it was accepted into the Buddhist canon.[3]

However, the more common theory among Buddhist scholars is that the *Book of Eights* is a Buddhist text that was composed early, perhaps originating in the first years of the Buddha's forty-five-year teaching career. It is fairly common for these scholars to assume the *Book of Eights* is among the earliest surviving teachings of the Buddha.[4] The lack of systematized, numerically ordered teachings is taken as evidence of its early composition. The ancient poetic meter in which some of the verses are composed further suggests an early date, as do some of the unusual and archaic words and word forms. The lack of any reference to settled monastic life also suggests that it may have been composed soon after the Buddha's awakening, while he and his monastic followers were peripatetic mendicants.

The most compelling evidence for the antiquity of the *Book of Eights,* however, is the fact that it is mentioned by name in three ancient Buddhist scriptures. We can at least conclude that the *Book of Eights* predates these canonical texts. One of them provides a lengthy commentary on a verse explicitly identified as coming from the *Book of Eights.*[5] In nearly identical passages in the other two texts, the Buddha asks a monk named Soṇa to recite the Dharma—that is, the teachings. Soṇa does so by reciting "all sixteen parts of the *Book of Eights.*"[6] The Buddha then congratulates Soṇa for his clear, well-delivered recitation. From this reference, it seems that the *Book of Eights* was already assembled at a very early date into the sixteen chapters we have today. It also shows that the anthology existed as an independent work at that time.

Preserving the Dharma

The *Soṇa Sutta* is also significant in providing evidence of the ancient Buddhist practice of using poetry to preserve, learn, and disseminate important teachings. A close connection between Buddhist teachings and poetry has existed from the very beginning of the religion. The ancient Buddhist scriptures state that the Buddha's first words after his enlightenment were expressed in verse.[7] These scriptures contain hundreds of poems and thousands of verses used to convey the teachings. Some of the poems stand alone, as they do in the *Book of Eights.* Other poems appear either interspersed in prose passages or, emphatically, at the end of prose teachings as a way to reiterate an important teaching.

The earliest surviving reports of how the Buddha and his disciples intentionally preserved and transmitted his teachings depict them using poetry. The story of Soṇa's recitation of the *Book of Eights* is an example of how verse was an accepted, perhaps even expected, means of conveying the teachings.

The *Book of Eights* has, within itself, evidence that it was recited. A quarter of the way through the twenty verses of "The Discourse on Being Violent," the existing text has an ancient editorial addition indicating that the verses should be recited. This was likely a communal recitation following the recitation of the opening verses by a single chanter.

It is safe to assume that any teachings that were intentionally composed, memorized, and recited as poetry were particularly valued by early Buddhists. Rather than relying on modern interpretations for what may have been these important teachings, the poems give voice to something the early Buddhists emphasized themselves.

In addition to the *Book of Eights,* the early scriptures contain a poem called "An Auspicious Day" and another anthology of poems called the *Book of the Way to the Other*

Shore (*Pārāyanavagga*) that canonical evidence suggests were also used for memorization, recitation, and teaching by the Buddha's followers. Together with the *Book of Eights,* these texts all reveal a common doctrine that is distinct from the standard presentations of early Buddhist teachings. All three of them also functioned as liturgy for recitation, verses for instruction, and means of preserving important teachings. The significance given to these poems is also seen in the reference to laypeople who had memorized either parts or all of the two anthologies. For example, according to the *Nandamātā Sutta,* a laywoman named Nandamātā recites the *Book of the Way to the Other Shore* to herself.[8]

"An Auspicious Day" is found in the *Middle Length Discourses,* one of five large anthologies of scriptures attributed to the Buddha and his immediate disciples.[9] The popularity of this poem is suggested by the fact that it occurs nine times in four different scriptures (texts usually referred to as *suttas,* or "discourses") in this anthology. Two of these discourses also contain commentaries on the poem, evidence that the Buddha and his monastic disciples used the poem as a basis for teaching. The explicit expectation that the Buddha's monastic disciples should memorize it further suggests that "An Auspicious Day" functioned as part of the disciples' education. Here is the poem:

AN AUSPICIOUS DAY

Don't chase the past
    Or long for the future.

The past is left behind;
The future is not yet reached.

Have insight into whatever phenomenon are present,
Right where it is;
Not faltering and not agitated,
By knowing whatever is present
One develops the mind.

Ardently do what should be done today—
Who knows, death may come tomorrow.
There is no bargaining with Mortality
And his great army.

Whoever dwells thus ardent,
—active day and night—
Is, says the peaceful sage,
One who has an auspicious day.

Except perhaps for the reference to Mortality's great army, the teachings in this poem are remarkably timeless. They are as relevant to us in the modern world as they probably were when they were composed twenty-five hundred years ago. The poem contains no ideology, sectarian beliefs, or reference to divine or supernatural realities. Instead it emphasizes attaining insight into the immediacy of one's present experience, an activity that gives one an "auspicious day." The reference to a "peaceful sage" suggests that peace is the desired attainment.

Because "An Auspicious Day" is a single, short poem,

we shouldn't use it alone to come to conclusions about early Buddhist teachings. However, together with the *Book of Eights,* the poem begins to reveal a pattern in the kind of teachings the early Buddhists memorized, recited, and taught one another.

This pattern is also seen in the *Book of the Way to the Other Shore.* The simplicity and directness of this anthology are represented by the following verses:

> Subdue greed for sensual pleasure.
> See renunciation as peace.
> Let there be nothing
> You take up or reject.
>
> Let what was in the past fade away,
> Make nothing of the future.
> If you don't cling to what is in the present,
> You can wander about calm.
>
> (verses 1098–1099)

The teachings in the *Book of the Way to the Other Shore* are related to those in the *Book of Eights,* as they too lack the systemized, analytical, and numerically organized teachings that are commonly associated with the Buddha and early Buddhism. Both texts emphasize attaining peace through not clinging to anything. Both refer to the person who does this as a sage (*muni*).

While the *Book of Eights,* the *Book of the Way to the Other Shore,* and "An Auspicious Day" are doctrinally distinct from what is found in many of the other early Buddhist scriptures, we should not assume they were outliers without any central importance. The evidence suggests the opposite; the stories of people memorizing, reciting, and explicating these three works suggest that they had an active role within early Buddhist communities. In fact, it may well be that these teachings lay at the heart of the earliest tradition. Many of the rest of the surviving teachings could be considered elaborations, adaptations, and digressions from these early foundational teachings.

Four Themes of the *Book of Eights*

Four basic themes are prominent in the teachings in the *Book of Eights*: letting go of views, avoiding sensual craving, the qualities of a sage, and the training to become a sage. The first two themes are the behaviors most associated with peace and nonclinging. The last two refer to the person who has attained these ideals and the practices that led to their attainment. Not all of these themes are in every poem, and some poems emphasize them more than others do.

Letting Go of Views (Chapters 3, 4, 5, 8, 9, 11, 12, and 13)

The predominant teaching regarding views is the importance of not clinging to any opinions, philosophies, doctrines, or religious teachings. This includes views about ultimate religious truth. The text teaches that to find peace, a follower should shake off every view without embracing or rejecting anything—this includes views about views. A number of verses are critical of any assertion that one's own religious beliefs are the truest or best, while others' are inferior.

For many readers, this seeming no-view teaching is a radical message. It undermines the importance of doctrines that underlie many religious traditions, including some Buddhist ones. The teachings in the *Book of Eights* provide no support for the idea that one should believe teachings just because they are found in certain Buddhist texts.

The poems include many examples of the problems that arise if one clings to views: attachment to concepts leads to debates and quarrels; it causes one to seek praise and leaves one feeling depressed when one's opinion is refuted; it causes one to swing between feeling high and low, depending on whether one is praised or criticized; and if clinging to views does bring a type of peace, it turns out to be an unstable one. Overall, the *Book of Eights* emphasizes that clinging to views does not lead to reliable peace.

Finally, the goal of practice is often described in terms of letting go of views. Those who have realized the goal—the sages—are not attached to views and so avoid debates, quarrels, and any conceit that their views are better than others. Letting go of their attachments, sages have no need for any doctrine in terms of theories, abstract concepts, or beliefs. With no reliance on such doctrines, the wise person does not oppose anyone else's doctrine. This is stated explicitly in the following verse:

They are not an enemy to any doctrine
  Seen, heard, or thought out.

Not forming opinions, not shut down, and not desirous,
They are sages, wise ones who have laid their burden down.

(verse 914)

The text does not explain what the "burden" is; in context, we can assume it refers to some attachment a person clings to and carries unnecessarily. "The Discourse to Māgaṇḍiya" (Chapter 9) contains a story of a person for whom the idea of letting go of religious views and theories is confusing. Because most religions are based on a particular doctrine, what are the faithful left with when they lay down their views? How can one hold a belief that's not in opposition to the doctrines of others?

The *Middle Length Discourses* answers these questions in a text where the Buddha states that his teachings are not the basis for debates and disagreements. Composed in prose rather than verse, the first part of this discourse, the Honeyball Sutta, shares so many concepts and so much vocabulary with the *Book of Eights* that the two were undoubtedly composed in the same milieu. The discourse begins with a man named Daṇḍapāṇi aggressively asking the Buddha to explain his teaching. It may be that Daṇḍapāṇi was interested in engaging the Buddha in a debate, an activity the *Book of Eights* considers pointless. Daṇḍapāṇi was left silent and bewildered when the Buddha replied,

> Such a teaching with which one does not quarrel with anyone in this world . . . [a teaching where a person] who lives uninvolved with lust and who is free of doubt, worry and craving for any existence does not cling to concepts. This is what I teach.[10]

Rather than teaching a doctrine that can be debated, the Buddha here teaches the importance of not clinging to concepts. In other words, he is not interested in doctrines as much as how people relate to them. Freedom isn't found through doctrines, though it does require not clinging to them.

After the Buddha explains his teachings, Daṇḍapāṇi leaves without saying anything further. However, some of the Buddha's monks ask him to elaborate on his statement. The Buddha then states,

> As for the basis on which conceptual differentiation, concepts, and conceptualizations occur, if there is nothing there to delight in, to welcome, or to be bound up with, this is the end to the obsessions with lust, aversion, views, doubt, conceit, ignorance, and the desire for becoming. That is the end of resorting to weapons, arguments, quarrels, disputes, accusations, divisive tale-bearing, and false speech. This is how malicious, unskillful states cease completely.[11]

The assumption in this statement is that if one looks underneath concepts at what they represent and finds nothing to be attached to, then one would not have any obsessions or tendencies toward unskillful states. This is described in terms of no longer getting involved in conflict. As with the *Book of Eights,* the Honeyball Sutta has a keen interest in preventing interpersonal conflict.

Attachment to views and doctrines is an obstacle to peace. When the attachment leads to conflict with others who hold different views, interpersonal peace is lost.

When the clinging brings mental agitation, inner peace is absent. For the *Book of Eights,* one of the important means to peace is to give up clinging to views and doctrines, especially the beliefs about ultimate religious truths, experiences, or realities.

Sensual Craving (Chapters 1, 2, 7, and 9)

The issue of sensual desire and sensual pleasure is another of the primary themes in the *Book of Eights.* In a sense, this theme is the entry point into the text as it's the subject of the first discourse in the collection, the *Kāma Sutta.* Anyone familiar with the renowned Indian sex manual with the same name, the *Kāma Sūtra* (*sūtra* being the Sanskrit word for the Pali equivalent, *sutta,* or "discourse"), will be struck by how distinctly these two texts stand in contrast to each other. The Sanskrit text teaches how to maximize sensual pleasure, while the much shorter Buddhist text teaches the dangers found in the *greed* for sensual pleasures. Through this greed, one will "be overcome by weakness, crushed by dangers, and penetrated by suffering as water penetrates a cracked boat." Sensual craving involves greed for anything experienced through the five physical senses. The poem lists an extensive range of items that can be the object of sensual desire, including "fields, property, cows and horses, servants, women, relatives."

The spiritual life championed by the *Book of Eights* is one that is not tied to the world of sense pleasure. As long as one is entangled in this world, one will not be free. In the language of the text, mental seclusion (*viveka)*—an important concept in early Buddhism—depends on letting go of sensual desires. For a modern English-speaking audience, the importance of this word might be better understood if *viveka* were rendered as "independence" and the sage as becoming independent of sensual desires.

The theme of avoiding sensual craving is sometimes stated in strong terms, for example in this verse from the first chapter:

> Sidestepping sensual desire
> —As one would the head of a snake with one's
> foot—
> Is the mindful one, who,
> While in this world, steps beyond craving.
>
> (verse 768)

Readers might conclude that the *Book of Eights* has an excessively negative view of sensual pleasures. However, I believe the main emphasis is not the pleasures themselves but rather the way people are caught up in sensual pursuits. The text describes this entanglement in many ways—such as being tied to, bound to, greedy for, intent on, and infatuated with sensual pleasures. If one is to reach the goal of the Buddhist path, one must no longer be in the grip of such pursuits:

> A person, ever mindful,
> Therefore turns away from sensual desires;
> Abandoning them, one will cross the flood,
> Like bailing a boat to reach the far shore.
>
> (verse 771)

The attachment to sexual intercourse is singled out as a particularly strong form of sensual desire. The entire "Discourse to Tissa Metteyya" (Chapter 7) is devoted to discussing the dangers that come with being addicted to sex. Perhaps surprisingly, given the strong emphasis on being independent without clinging to anything, most of the dangers mentioned have to do with receiving other people's disapproval.

It is not just attachment to sex that is to be avoided; the "Discourse to Tissa Metteyya" explicitly counsels celibacy. For this poem, the dangers of sexual activity are avoided by not engaging in sex. It is possible that these teachings are based on the premise that it is not possible to engage in sexual activity without having some attachment. To be free of attachments thus means becoming celibate. For modern lay readers, celibacy may be challenging and unwelcome. However, rather than rejecting this teaching outright, laypeople could be inspired to explore any attachments or cravings they might have regarding sex.

Description of the Sage (Chapters 4, 6, 9, 10, 13, and 15)

A third theme in the *Book of Eights* is the qualities of the sage. Due to the sage's proficiency in realizing peace, he or she is often referred to as "a skilled person" or "expert" (*kusalo*). In that sages are wise, they are also referred to as "the wise one" (*dhiro*), "the learned one" (*pandito*), and "one of much wisdom" (*bhuri paňňo*). With the shedding of attachment, this person is also called "the cleansed one" (*dhono*). In some passages, the word *brahmin* is used to describe the sage. At the time of the Buddha, brahmins were a hereditary social class that considered itself superior to all other classes. In using the title for a sage, the text is appropriating or redefining the term so it no longer refers to the social class. A "true brahmin" is someone who has let go of all of his or her clinging.

In many passages describing the goal of peace, the *Book of Eights* emphasizes the skillful sage's behavior rather than an attainment distinct from how he or she lives. For example, with the possible exception of the enigmatic verse 874, the text does not mention any singular attainment or transcendent and extraordinary states of consciousness. No mention is made of psychic powers such as the divine eye or the divine ear that are important in other early Buddhist discourses. Rather, the text enumerates the ethical behaviors in which such people would or would not engage and the qualities of inner virtue or character they would possess. In this way, the religious goal of the texts is always described in ordinary human terms, not in mystical, transcendent, or metaphysical terms.

The most common attribute associated with a sage is peace (*santi*). Such a person advocates peace, sees and knows peace, is at peace, and is peaceful. The sage is also tranquil, still and unmoving, unshakable, and equanimous. Though peace is clearly an attribute of sages, they do not *depend* on peace or intentionally take it up. This is because sages do not depend on or take up anything; instead, they let go.

These designations and descriptions of the adept suggest qualities that can be discerned in oneself and that are directly relevant to how one lives one's life. They do not suggest that the sage has psychic or supernormal powers or has attained transcendent realities removed from this world. Instead, they point to a pragmatic, observable mode of being in the world.

A significant attribute of skillful sages is their ability to know and see—sometimes they are called the "ones who know." They do not see the nature of ultimate reality or some form of ultimate consciousness. Rather, sages know and see the ways in which people struggle. They know what is not harmonious and what is dangerous. They know the problems that come from pride and holding on to opinions. They see how people selfishly thrash about, get elated and deflated in their disputes, speak with arrogance, and cling to teachings. By having insights into these afflictive states, a wise person knows not to get involved with them and to let go of them. The appendix of this book gathers quotes of many of the positive references to knowing and seeing in the *Book of Eights*. Seeing these excerpts together provides an overview of how important these activities were for the composers of the text.

Being at peace and having overcome cravings, sages become independent in knowing the Dharma through their own direct insight and experience. They don't depend on anything, including doctrines, precepts, and religious observances.

In discussing the sage, the *Book of Eights* does not use the more familiar words or titles that are common in other, probably later, Buddhist texts. For example, in contrast to many of the canonical Buddhist discourses, nowhere in the *Book of Eights* is the ideal person called an *arahant.* Literally meaning a "worthy one," this title refers to the notion that the ideal person is worthy of respect and offerings. *Arahant* is therefore a description of how the sage is to be treated by others. All the words used to describe the ideal person in the *Book of Eights* refer to his or her personal qualities. The emphasis is on the character and behavior of individuals, not on what or how the person is in relation to others.

Also absent is any reference to people being stream-enterers, once-returners, and nonreturners. The terms *once-returner* and *nonreturner* refer to the concept of rebirth. Once-returners have attained such a degree of spiritual liberation that they will only be reborn as a human being one more time. Nonreturners, having a higher degree of liberation, are not reborn again as humans. Instead, after death, they appear in a heavenly realm where they attain their full liberation. Because rebirth has no role in the teachings of the *Book of Eights,* it's not surprising that the concepts of rebirth are not used in reference to accomplished practitioners, those people who are referred to as peaceful, wise, learned, skilled, and cleansed.

Training (Chapters 14, 15, and 16)

A fourth theme of the *Book of Eights* is that of training, or the practices conducive to peace and becoming a sage. While all the chapters of the *Book of Eights* discuss what someone on the path should and should not do, the last three chapters give the most attention to this theme.

The *Book of Eights* focuses on fundamental, personal, and psychological transformations for which individuals are personally responsible: "Train fully in your own release" (verse 940) and "A monastic wouldn't seek peace from others" (verse 919). The text provides no help from gods or external forces. To many modern readers, this will be less of a revolutionary message than it probably was in the Buddha's time.

In focusing on cultivating behaviors and virtues, the *Book of Eights* rarely mentions specific techniques or practices. Stated differently, the text doesn't emphasize religious practices that can be seen as steps toward attaining the qualities of the ideal person. Furthermore, it explicitly and provocatively says that religious observances and practices in themselves are not adequate for becoming a person at peace. Rather, it encourages people to simply behave like the ideal sage.

There is no sharp distinction between the means and the goal in the *Book of Eights.* That is, the personal qualities of someone who has attained the goal are the same qualities one is to cultivate when training for the goal. One trains by being what one is to become. If the goal is to be peaceful, the way there is to be peaceful. If the goal is to be released from craving, the way there is to "train to subdue their cravings" (verse 916). In this way the achievement of the goal is not radically distinct from what led to that achievement.

The emphasis on training in chapters 14, 15, and 16 is different enough from the themes of the earlier chapters to give the impression that the former were composed within a different context, perhaps for a different audience. They may have been composed later than the earlier poems, and their placement at the end of the anthology gives some support to the idea that they were added last. Whereas the earlier poems give no indication of the existence of a Buddhist monastic community, chapters 14 and 16, in particular, are explicitly directed toward monastics.

Purity versus Peace

While peace is the most commonly mentioned Buddhist goal in the *Book of Eights,* "purity" (*suddhi*) is the most frequent word used for the goal of non-Buddhists. There are no references in the text to suggest that the Buddha explicitly approves of any statements that define purity as the ultimate goal.[12] Of the twenty-three uses of the word *purity,* ten occur in descriptions the Buddha gives for beliefs non-Buddhists have about their ideal goal.[13] In five other occurrences, he uses the word in response to what others say or ask about it.[14] While he does not explicitly reject the concept, it is not how he prefers to describe the goal. In one verse where the Buddha is willing to use the word *purity* in relationship to the ultimate goal, he only explains what purity is not. But then he seems to drop the reference to purity as he goes on to say that the goal is attained through letting go (verse 839). In one other passage, he seems to accept purity indirectly as a label for the goal but only by again describing it as the absence of grasping (verse 876).

The Buddha's strongest affirmative reference to purity is in verse 834, where he describes himself as pure. Except for this, nowhere does the *Book of Eights* directly discuss the Buddhist goal, or the qualities of someone who has attained that goal, in terms of purity. In fact, a sage doesn't wish for purity (verse 813), doesn't have "wishes for 'purity' or 'impurity'" (verse 900), and doesn't see anything in terms of "absolute purity" (verse 794). It would seem that the sage should let go of any concern with purity.

As already noted, the Buddha's preferred way of referring to the ideal goal is peace (*santi*). He commonly describes those who have realized this goal as peaceful.[15] They are "peaceful among those not at peace" (verse 912). They know that release—that is, being free of clinging—is peace (verse 933).

This contrast between the uses of *purity* and *peace* represent a difference in religious goals and values between the Buddha and other religious practitioners of the time. It also suggests that to better understand the *Book of Eights,* we have to understand the religious context in which it was composed.

Religious Context for the *Book of Eights*

The first generations of Indian Buddhists lived in an environment heavily defined by the religious beliefs, practices, and values of the brahmins and the renunciants. As with the early Buddhist literature in general, these two types of religious practitioners are mentioned repeatedly in the *Book of Eights.*[16] While ancient Buddhists commonly distinguished themselves from the brahmins and renunciants, they also shared many ideas with these fellow religious practitioners.

Brahmins were a hereditary group that considered

themselves the superior social class. Some were wealthy landowners, and others were the priests responsible for preserving their sacred teachings and conducting rituals. Purity was a central concern of the brahmins, and the careful observances of rituals and social taboos were important means for attaining purity. The first poem in the *Book of Eights* lists the kind of possessions associated with wealthy people of the times, including rich male brahmins: fields, goods, gold, cows, horses, servants, women, relatives, and lots of sensual pleasures.

The orthodox brahmin priests adhered to the old Vedic religion based on the *Rig-Veda* and its commentaries, some of which date back before 1000 B.C.E. In the century or two before the Buddha, a new movement evolved out of the old religion and focused more on personal transformation and realization than the performance of rituals and prayers to the gods. The new movement seems to have been strongly associated with groups of renunciants. It often criticized, downplayed, or reinterpreted the rituals and symbols of the brahmins. An important body of literature for some renunciant groups was the Upanishads. These are sacred texts, some of which claim to contain teachings of particular sages who lived prior to the Buddha.

Renunciants were a group of diverse religious seekers who renounced ordinary, domestic lifestyles for lives of radical simplicity and poverty. The common Buddhist term for such a person is *samaṇa,* a word that may originally have meant "striver," but which I have rendered as "renunciant" to convey a characteristic feature of their lifestyle. Other translators have often translated the word as "ascetic" or "recluse." Most commonly, *samaṇas* renounced possessions and sexual activity. Because they lived without a fixed residence, they were sometimes called "homeless." While renunciants often shared similar lifestyles in giving up domestic life to become full-time religious practitioners, their actual beliefs and practices were quite diverse. Most commonly they were associated with asceticism, meditation, and/or doctrinal speculation, with some specializing in one of these topics more than others.

Buddhist monastics belonged to this renunciant group, sometimes identifying themselves as *samaṇas,* but more commonly referring to themselves with as *bhikkhus.* Literally meaning "mendicant," *bhikkhu* refers to the practice of relying on alms for food and other necessities. The Buddha and his early followers shared many practices and ideas with other renunciants. One of the clearest ways to see this is through the ideas the Buddhist texts share with the early Upanishads.

Many concepts that are now identified as Buddhist were already current in these early Vedic treatises. This is especially the case with the *Upanishad of the Great Forest* (*Bṛhadāraṇyaka Upaniṣad*), a text that maybeen composed and known in the part of India where the Buddha lived. Consistent with early Buddhism, this Upanishad teaches the attainment of realization through letting go of all desires. Also similar to early Buddhism, it describes realization in terms of overcoming sorrow, delusion, old age, and death.[17] Furthermore, as in Buddhism, the *Upanishad of the Great Forest* espouses the idea of renouncing lay life to become a *bhikkhu*.[18] Its teachings on karma and rebirth are also similar to what is found in Buddhist texts.[19]

We see then that some Buddhist ideas are less a break from the earlier Upanishadic tradition than a continuation or modification of it. To highlight the distinctions without acknowledging the similarities obscures the context from which early Buddhist teachings arose. In relation to the *Book of Eights,* this means we can better understand some of its poems in light of the teachings of the Upanishads, especially the *Upanishad of the Great Forest.* This is particularly true for "The Discourse on Quarrels and Disputes" (Chapter 11), a text that is difficult to understand without the help of the *Upanishad of the Great Forest.* For example, the answers the Buddha provides may use words and concepts in the way the Upanishadic interlocutor understands them, not the way later Buddhists did.[20]

Buddhist Context for the *Book of Eights*

Chapters 14 and 16 of the *Book of Eights* are clearly placed in a Buddhist context in that they contain teachings intended for Buddhist monastics. This is particularly true in chapter 16 where the questioner is Sāriputta, one of the Buddha's foremost monastic disciples.[21]

The five verses attributed to Sāriputta contain different concepts and emphases than those found in the rest of the *Book of Eights.* In contrast to the Buddha's seeming reluctance to hold up purity as a desirable goal, Sāriputta asks what trainings one should undertake to purify oneself. In contrast to the here-and-now, this-world emphasis elsewhere in the text, Sāriputta mentions the unseen world of gods and heavenly realms. He also brings in a degree of respect, reverence, and praise for the Buddha not seen in the rest of the book. It is interesting that Sāriputta here utters the only occurrence of the title Buddha in the *Book of Eights*. Perhaps the verses attributed to him illustrate how the Buddha and his teachings were viewed by his disciples. As such, these verses may provide one example of how the Buddha's teachings were changed over time, first by his direct disciples and then by later followers. If we are interested in knowing what the Buddha actually taught, we have to be careful to distinguish his teachings from those of his disciples and from the later tradition.

We have one clear example of how one of the Buddha's preeminent monks interpreted a portion of the *Book of Eights*. In a collection of *suttas* called the *Connected Discourses,* a layperson recites a verse from the *Book of Eights* and then asks Venerable Mahā Kaccāna to explain its meaning. This verse, from a poem called "The Discourse to Māgaṇḍiya" (Chapter 9), is as follows:

> Letting go of home,
> Wandering without a household,
> Not becoming intimate with villagers
> Free from sensual desire,
> Free of expectations,
> A sage won't quarrel with people.
>
> (verse 844)

Mahā Kaccāna begins his explanation by interpreting *home* metaphorically, saying that if one has attachments to one's body (*rūpadhātu*), consciousness will be stuck at home with the body:

> The body, Householder, is the home of consciousness; one whose consciousness is chained by lust for physicality is called one who wanders about in a home.
>
> SN 22.3; iii 9–10

Mahā Kaccāna goes on to state that if all attachments to physical experience are eliminated, consciousness will not be limited by anything and so will "wander homeless." This same metaphor is then applied to feeling, perception, and mental formations: if one doesn't cling to any of these, consciousness can also be considered homeless. Through this metaphorical interpretation, Mahā Kaccāna explains the first words of the verse so they are relevant for the layperson, meaning the householder who asked for the explanation.

Mahā Kaccāna takes a similar approach to interpret "wandering without a household." *Household* is defined as sense impressions. Someone who is attached to sense objects "wanders with a household"; someone without attachments to sense objects "wanders without a household."

Mahā Kaccāna provides descriptive explanations for the remaining lines of the poem. For example, for the line, "A sage won't quarrel with people," Mahā Kaccāna states,

> And how, Householder, does one not quarrel with people? Here, Householder, one does not speak with such talk as, "You do not understand this teaching and discipline! I understand this teaching and discipline. Your practice is wrong. My practice is right. . . . I am consistent. You are not consistent. . . . Your doctrine has been refuted. . . ." In this way one does not quarrel with people.
>
> SN 22:3; iii 12

This same passage occurs nine other times in various Pali discourses. Most likely, Mahā Kaccāna is interpreting the poem according to current established Buddhist teachings of his time. Rather than presenting his own interpretation, he engages the practice of finding or making meaning through establishing a connection between one teaching and another.

These two explanations by Mahā Kaccāna represent two different interpretative approaches. The first is contextual and innovative in offering a unique, metaphorical explanation that made a passage relevant for his audience. The second relies on having a good grasp of a range of Buddhist teachings and then establishing a connection of equivalence between two different canonical statements and concepts.

A version of this second approach is found in the *Mahāniddesa* (*The Great Explanation*), an early canonical commentary that explains each word in the *Book of Eights* by listing synonyms. Here we see the introduction of concepts that are absent from the Buddha's teachings in the *Book of Eights.* For example, in the *Mahāniddesa,* peace (*santi*)—the primary goal in the *Book of Eights*—is discussed in terms of a "state" (*pada*) of peace. Repeatedly, the text describes this state with concepts such as "the state of shelter, the state of safety, the state of refuge, the state of fearlessness, the eternal state, the deathless state, the state of *nibbāna.*"[22] Not only do these synonyms introduce concepts that aren't in the *Book of Eights,* such as eternity and deathlessness, but they also discuss peace in abstract terms as if it can be distinguished from a person who is peaceful. Overall, the idea of an actual peaceful sage recedes from view in the *Mahāniddesa.*

The abstract concept of a state of peace does appear once in the *Book of Eights.*[23] However, it isn't the Buddha who uses this expression, but one of his questioners. This person asks the Buddha what someone needs to see to become free and achieve a state of peace. In his response, the Buddha does not answer the question as it is asked. He makes no mention of what one needs to see to be free nor does he refer to a state of peace. Instead he describes the actions one would or would not take to become free and the inner experiences one would feel. For example, one would subdue one's craving and not get attached to any teachings. A person who did this would be tranquil and still.

The Buddha's avoidance here of discussing the spiritual ideal in terms of abstract, impersonal states highlights the very different direction the *Mahāniddesa* takes in introducing concepts like eternity or deathlessness. It is an example of how later Buddhism began to emphasize the transcendent state of liberation rather than the eminent qualities and behavior of a person who is liberated.

The *Book of Eights* in Action

An alternative to studying the meaning and interpretations of the teachings in the *Book of Eights* is to view the text as performative literature with aesthetic value designed to be recited and heard. In the early centuries of Buddhism in India, the teachings were not recorded in books. Instead they were memorized and recited. When sacred texts are repeatedly recited or chanted, they tend to have a different effect than if they are simply read for their content. When people recite a text, they activate their memory and voice. When the text is a poem with a meter, as is the case for the *Book of Eights* in its original language (Pali), people could feel physically connected to the rhythm of the poem's beat. In public performances, the quality of the recitation can be an important part of conveying the teachings. That this was valued in the ancient Buddhist world can be seen in the Buddha's response to Soṇa's recitation of the *Book of Eights*:

> Excellent! Excellent! Monk, you have learned well the sixteen [part] *Book of Eights,* you have remembered it well, have borne it well in mind. You spoke them in a lovely way, with good enunciation, and faultless so to make the meaning clear.
>
> *Soṇa Sutta*; *Udana* 5.6

Some scholars of the *Book of Eights* have called these discourses "ballads" rather than poems because they believe that in the ancient world the poems were sung more than chanted.[24] This idea comes partly from a passage in the *Sutta Nipāta,* the same anthology that includes the *Book of Eights,* where the Buddha mentions that he "sang" (*gīta*) a particular set of verses found in the *Sutta Nipāta.*[25] While it is not clear that *gīta* should be understood as "singing" in our modern English sense of the word, the term *gīta* does suggest a performative role for these poems. The impact of the meter, metaphors, and dialogue all contribute to an overall aesthetic experience for an audience listening to the "performance."

The idea that these poems are carefully crafted compositions used for the purpose of teaching reveals a different dimension of the text than would be revealed if one only studied the content of the *Book of Eights.* By the content alone, one interpretation of these teachings is that because they predominantly emphasize what one is to let go of and what one is not to do, they advocate nonaction and perhaps a radical noninvolvement in the world. But if the medium is part of the message, then these poems convey the value of composing, preserving, and presenting teachings for the welfare of others. In other words, the existence of these poems is evidence of a particular kind of engagement with the world.

Stories in the canon suggest that efforts were made to explicitly teach the *Book of Eights* to others. Specifically, two people in Avanti, a country in Western India far from the region where Buddhism was first established, are reported to have learned the *Book of Eights*. One is the layperson mentioned earlier who asked Mahā Kaccāna to explain verse 844. The second is the monk of Soṇa, who recited the *Book of Eights* for the Buddha only one year after becoming a fully ordained monk. Whoever taught these two people to memorize the *Book of Eights*—we can't know for sure, but most likely it was Mahā Kaccāna—presumably understood its teachings. Its thoroughgoing message of not clinging did not interfere with the effort to teach the text to others.

Translating the *Book of Eights*

I started this translation of the *Book of Eights* twenty years ago as a way to study a few of its discourses. Over the years, I gradually came to translate all sixteen discourses. Once those translations were complete, I spent years editing and, at times, revising the translations. In doing this, I was influenced by the work and suggestions of other translators and scholars of early Buddhism.

An important motivation for this work has been to understand the ancient Buddhist teachings as they might have been understood at the time they were composed. Rather than looking through the lens of a culture and a time far removed from those of the Buddha, I tried to interpret the texts in the context with which I believe the Buddha may have been familiar early in his teaching career. While I do not assume that I have succeeded at this task, the exercise itself has helped me to discover and put aside a number of modern interpretations about early Buddhist teachings.

As is the case for most translators, it is likely that my biases and cultural conditioning have influenced both my understanding and my translation choices. I don't underestimate the difficulty of understanding a culture from a time and place very different from my own. Undoubtedly I have not understood many of the nuances, references, and subtleties of meaning.

I have followed a number of principles in creating this translation. I have tried, to the best of my limited ability, to be faithful to the literal meaning of the Pali originals. At the same time, I also have tried to render the verses in English so they are easy to understand and pleasant to read. Finding the balance between being literal on the one hand and understandable and enjoyable on the other was never easy. One consequence of this choice was the decision not to try to replicate in English the meters in which the poems were composed.

The primary departure from a literal translation is the avoidance of the male pronouns by using gender-neutral words like *they* where the original text has "he." This required me, for example, to turn the occurrences of the singular "sage" into the plural "sages." In order to further produce a translation that was more gender neutral than the original, I translated *bhikkhu,* usually rendered into English as "monk," as the gender-neutral "monastic."

A translator often has a range of choices of English words to use for translating a Pali term. While a Pali-English dictionary may list several English words as meanings for the Pali, these words may each have different connotations that tilt the meaning and the mood of the translation in one direction or another. For example, verse 935, which I have translated and formatted as

> Violence gives birth to fear;
> [Just] look at people and [their] quarrels.
> I will speak of my dismay
> And the way that I was shaken.

is translated and formatted by K. R. Norman as

> Fear comes from the [one who has] embraced violence. Look at
> people quarrelling. I shall describe my agitation, how it was experienced by me.[26]

Hammalawa Saddhatissa translates it as

> Fear results from resorting to violence—just look at how
> People quarrel and fight! But let me tell you now of the kind of dismay and terror that I have felt.[27]

And Andrew Olendzki, replicating the ancient eight-beat meter, translates it as

> Fear is born from arming oneself.
> Just see how many people fight!
> I'll tell you about the dreadful fear
> that caused me to shake all over.[28]

What I have rendered as dismay (*saṃvega*), Norman has translated as "agitation," and Olendzki as "dreadful fear." And what I have translated as "shaken" (*saṃvijitaṃ*), Norman has translated as "experienced," Saddhatissa as either "terror" or "felt" (it is not clear), and Olendzki as "shake all over." While all these words represent the meanings of the Pali words accurately enough, their use in the translations results in a very different effect. Presumably the word choice reflects some understanding or preference of the translator. If this understanding or preference is used consistently throughout the translation, the sum total creates a different impression or tone from one version to another.

Sometimes I was reluctant to choose between different meanings, connotations, and moods provided by different English words. However, choices were made, and I am sure that my own preferences have skewed the translation more than I intended. My hope, however, is that my word choices point to the peace that is the goal championed by the Buddha and at the same time respect the ancient Buddhists who preserved and applied his teachings.

Reading the *Book of Eights*

As is often the case with poetry, the *Book of Eights* can be read and interpreted in many ways. One way to read the text is with the intention of discovering exactly what the Buddha taught. Some people have done this by taking literally every word in the text as a recording of what the Buddha spoke. Others have engaged in "textual archeology," trying to recover the passages that can reliably be attributed to him. Searching for what the Buddha actually taught is sometimes guided by the wish to learn what a great religious figure thought about what might be ultimately true—such as the purpose of life, who we are, or the highest states of realization. The *Book of Eights* challenges this approach because it counsels against looking for ultimate truth.

It is possible that to settle on a single interpretation of the poems might not have been the original intention of those who composed them. Another approach is therefore to read the poems as having a range of possible meanings, interpretations, and applications, as Mahā Kaccāna does in his commentary on verse 844. Some of the wordplay that appears in the Pali version of the poems lends itself to multiple meanings, which may not be apparent in English. For example, verse 853 refers to the ideal sages as faithless and not freeing themselves from passion. In a conventional sense, this statement is surprising, perhaps even shocking, as faith is often seen as the foundation of a religious life, and freedom from passion is understood to be a requirement for spiritual freedom. However, the claim is not surprising if we realize that someone who has realized peace has no more need for faith in a path to peace. Those who are free of passion have no need to free themselves further.

For anyone interested in the peace advocated in the *Book of Eights,* one of the most productive ways of reading is to consider how the poems may be relevant in helping us to be more peaceful. Rather than agreeing or disagreeing with a teaching and rather than liking or not liking a poem, we can try to discover the particular circumstances where it may apply to us. For the purposes of peace, evaluating the text by personal preferences and opinions is less useful than doing the work to find how they might be of benefit to ourselves and others. Certainly there is no peace in arguing about the truth found in the *Book of Eights.*

Notes

Text placed in parentheses indicates that the material represents an ancient editorial note preserved in the extant Pali edition. Text placed in square brackets indicates that the material is my addition to the translation added for the purpose of clarity.

The numbering assigned to each verse is based on the Pali language edition of the *Sutta Nipāta* edited by Dines Andersen and Helmer Smith (Pali Text Society, 1913, 1990). While this Pali edition starts its numbering of the first verse of the *Book of Eights* with 766, the Myanmar edition of the Pali text begins with 772. The numbers in the two versions thus differ by six.

CHAPTER I

The Discourse on Desire

Sidestepping Sensual Desire

The *Book of Eights* begins, in its first chapter, with a teaching on the avoidance of sensual desire, greed, and craving. While "The Discourse on Desire" acknowledges that obtaining the object of one's sensual desire can be a joy, it emphasizes the piercing pain that can come when the pleasure fades away. Given this intimate connection between sensual desire and suffering, if one hopes to avoid suffering, one must avoid sensual desire. These ideas are presented in the poem through the use of strong and evocative metaphors. A dangerous snake is used to represent sensual desires. Water pouring into a leaking boat signifies the way greed brings about trouble and suffering. It is only by abandoning desire—bailing out the water—that one can cross the floods of desire to the safety of the far shore.

The metaphor of crossing occurs five separate times in the *Book of Eights*.[1] In this first occurrence, crossing is linked to safety. Safety does not come from fixing the leaky boat, because even if the boat is fixed, one remains in dangerous waters, subject to future challenges. Instead, safety is found by going beyond the floods—that is, by no longer having sensual desire.

The word translated here as "sensual desire" is *kāma,* a word occurring six times in this poem, including in the title, the *Kāma Sutta.* The word has three closely related meanings: it can refer to desire in general, to desire for specific sense pleasures, or to the sense pleasures themselves—the objects of sense desires. Only by understanding the particular context in which the word appears can we know which of these three meanings are intended. All three are found in the *Kāma Sutta.* When referring to sensual desire, the word has such strong connotations that it could also be translated as "lust."

Ideas about *kāma* were important in ancient Indian religious teachings, although there was a general division between two distinct views. Some traditions embraced *kāma* as an important and appropriate pursuit of human life, while others taught that it should be avoided. The opening chapter of the *Book of Eights* clearly falls in the latter camp. When the poem states that worldly items such as fields, goods, gold, cows, horses, servants, women, relatives, and sensual pleasures bring troubles and should be abandoned, it was undoubtedly creating a clear contrast with the male brahmins, the upper class of Vedic priests, who considered these pursuits to be one of the goals of life.

The Indian division between those who viewed *kāma* as a valued part of life and those who denounced it can be seen clearly in the contrast between the opening chapter of the *Book of Eights,* titled the *Kāma Sutta,* and the better-known Sanskrit book with the same title (the *Kāma Sūtra*). The Sanskrit work teaches that the pleasures of the arts, including the sexual arts, are one of the three worthy goals of human life.[2]

In the "Discourse on Desire," *kāma* is something to be avoided. This teaching is not unique to early Buddhism; earlier ascetically inclined religious movements also emphasized avoiding cravings. For example, the ultimate goal in the *Bṛhadāraṇyaka Upaniṣad*—described both as becoming immortal and attaining ultimate reality—is achieved when one is freed from all *kāma.*[3] What differentiates the "Discourse on Desire" from the earlier literature is the former's strong emphasis on the inherent problems of *kāma*. In the *Bṛhadāraṇyaka Upaniṣad* (2.4.2), becoming immortal is what motivates the renunciation of wealth and the household life. But in the "Discourse on Desire," there is no claim of an ultimate, permanent state. Instead the motivation for letting go is the wish to become safe from danger.

Kāma Sutta
The Discourse on Desire

When desire for sensual pleasure
  Is fulfilled
  One will surely be delighted.
  —The mortal's obtained what the mortal wanted.

[766]

But if this pleasure fades away,
The person with this desire,
—Who gives birth to this desire—
Is pained as if pierced by an arrow.

[767]

Sidestepping sensual desire
—As one would the head of a snake with one's
foot—
Is the mindful one, who,
While in this world, steps beyond craving.

[768]

Through greed for fields, goods,
Gold, cows and horses,
Servants, women, relatives,
And lots of sensual pleasures,

[769]

One's weakness overpowers;
Crushed by many troubles,
Suffering pours in
As water into a leaking boat.

[770][4]

A person, ever mindful,
Therefore turns away from sensual desires;
Abandoning them, one will cross the flood,
Like bailing a boat to reach the far shore.

[771]

CHAPTER 2

The Eightfold Discourse on the Hiding Place

Seclusion from Entanglement

The second chapter of the *Book of Eights*, "The Eightfold Discourse on the Hiding Place," continues with the theme of desire (*kāma*) begun in the preceding poem. Here, too, we encounter the metaphor of the arrow, which represents the piercing pain of desire, and the image of crossing rising waters, which signifies going beyond desire to freedom. The poem's depiction of *kāma* as something to be avoided is emphasized by the use of "hunger," "thirst," "greed," and "attachment" as near-synonyms for this form of desire. While the preceding discourse focuses on worldly desires for sense pleasures, possessions, and people, this poem introduces existential desires—for becoming and nonbecoming (*bhava* and *abhava*).

In most instances, I have translated *bhava* as "becoming." The word *bhava* is derived from the root *bhū,* meaning "to become." Because early Buddhism viewed life (including multiple lifetimes) as a continuing process of change, translating *bhava* as "becoming" seems particularly apt. Some translators, however, prefer to render it as "existence" and *abhava* as "nonexistence." I opted for this translation in verse 773.

In this poem, as well as elsewhere in the *Book of Eights,* context helps determine whether becoming refers solely to one's current lifetime or to states of existence over many subsequent lifetimes. When reporting on what other people believe, becoming often refers to rebirth. When the narrator of the poem—presumably the Buddha—is speaking directly, the word more often refers to states of becoming in one's lifetime here and now.

For those who believe in rebirth, the craving to "become" in a next life leads to misery, grief, and worries about what will happen when they are about to die. Those who have crossed the flood and become free from clinging, however, will be free of this anguish. They will "not long for this world or the next."

Whether "becoming" is understood to refer to states of identification in a single lifetime or over a series of lives, the source of freedom is the same: understanding the nature and functioning of "sensory experience" and "concepts." This emphasis on sensory experience and conceptualization suggests that freedom can be found in the immediacy of one's present-moment experience. People can only cling to things through their perceptions and conceptions of those things. When we cling, we grasp our perceptions and concepts, not the things themselves. The moment we stop grasping the perceptions and concepts, clinging ends. When this is fully and completely understood, a person will not have desires for "this world or the next" (verse 779).

People who crave states of becoming or nonbecoming —existence or nonexistence—are described as "thrashing about," an idea reinforced with the powerful metaphor of fish flailing in shallow water. This water that people struggle in is selfishness, their concepts of what is "me" or "mine." To live without clinging to self is to live without clinging to any states of becoming. It is also to be free from anxiety about what will happen at the moment of death.

In the first stanza, the poem contrasts hiding with seclusion. The act of physically or mentally removing oneself, hiding from the temptations of the world, is not a solution to the problem of suffering if one remains confused and filled with desires. Seclusion (*viveka*), on the other hand, refers to a freedom from desire that's arrived at by understanding the primary objects of clinging: sense experience and concepts. The word *seclusion* suggests a kind of integrity and disentanglement in the face of the world and all its temptations.

The last two verses are the first in the *Book of Eights* to describe the qualities of the ideal sage, a person who has attained the goal championed in the text. Many of the verses in the anthology continue this theme. An important point about this ideal that's emphasized in "The Eightfold Discourse on the Hiding Place" is that "one isn't liberated by others." Each person must realize the goal alone. Having done so, one has crossed the flood of sensual desire and removed the arrow of craving.

Guhaṭṭhaka Sutta
The Eightfold Discourse on the Hiding Place

For someone sunk in confusion,
—Even if well concealed in a hiding place—
Seclusion is far away.[1]
In this world, it's not easy to let go of desires!

[772]

Hard to free
Are those tied to wishes
And bound to the charm of existence.
Surely, one isn't liberated by others!

Longing for what has been and what can be,
They hunger for sensual pleasures that they've had.
Greedy, stingy, attached, and obsessed with desires,
They are wedded to disharmony.[2]

Presented with suffering, they lament,
"What will become of us when we pass away from
here?"

[773–74]

Therefore you should train right here:
Don't do what you know
is out of harmony in the world—
Life is short, say the wise.

[775]

I see people thrashing about in the world,
Thirsting for states of existence.[3]
Not freed from craving becoming and nonbecoming,
Lowly people weep in the face of death.

[776]

See them thrashing about in their selfishness,[4]
Like fish in tiny puddles of a drying stream.
Observing this, live unselfishly,
Not forming attachments to becoming.

[777]

Subduing desire for both sides,[5]
Fully understanding sense experience,[6]
Free of greed,
And doing nothing one would reproach oneself for,
A sage does not attach to what is seen or heard.

[778]

Fully understanding concepts[7] and having crossed the flood
Sages don't cling to possessions.
With arrow removed, living alertly,
They do not long for this world or the next.

[779]

CHAPTER 3

The Eightfold Discourse on the Corrupt

Shaking Off Every View

"The Eightfold Discourse on the Corrupt" is the first discourse in the *Book of Eights* to address the issue of philosophical or religious views. The poem gives the impression of having been composed in a climate of intense doctrinal debates and disagreements. Rather than participating in these disputes by arguing for or against any particular view, this third discourse focuses on the ways people relate to religious doctrines—looking specifically at the motivations behind people's views and their attachments to these views.

According to this discourse, desires and preferences can be tangled up with one's spiritual beliefs. That is, people sometimes hold particular views because doing so is to their advantage. Yet rather than providing any lasting advantage or pleasure, the satisfactions that come from being entangled in doctrines are inherently unstable. And because they're unstable, those who argue over doctrines can become despondent when their beliefs don't hold up in debates. Even when a person is being honest and sincere, arguing over doctrines can be destructive.

The main point of this discourse is the importance of becoming unattached to views and doctrines. The text offers the radical message that the person who is unattached has no need for views—or as the last verse states, "has shaken off every view." In particular, such a person does not form views about states of becoming or nonbecoming.

As we saw in the previous discourse, the terms *becoming* and *nonbecoming* can refer both to future states of existence and to the identities and conceits people assume in their current lives. This discourse doesn't offer a clear indication as to which of these meanings is being used here. It could be future lifetimes, or it might be the one right now.

The last verse ends emphatically with the statement that the ideal person has shaken off views "right here." Thus the goal advocated in the *Book of Eights* is not found in future lifetimes. It is clearly attainable here and now, in this lifetime and in this world. This idea is reinforced by the repeated and explicit mention of the "world" (*loka*) as the location in which the teachings apply.[1] In fact, the doctrine of multiple lifetimes and other future worlds, a central feature of much of Indian Buddhism, has little role in the *Book of Eights*—except as something a sage doesn't form views about. This may be implied by the line, "Those who are cleansed do not form a view about states of becoming or nonbecoming anywhere in the world."

Duṭṭhaṭṭhaka Sutta
The Eightfold Discourse on the Corrupt

Some dispute with their minds corrupt;
Some dispute with truthful minds.
Sages do not enter disputes that have arisen
And so do not become despondent anywhere.[2]

[780]

As one knows, so one speaks:
How could one overcome one's views
When led by desire, stuck in what's pleasing,
And making up [ideas of] what's correct?

[781]

Of ignoble character—say the skillful [ones]—
Is someone who, unasked, boasts
Of one's self, and
Of one's virtue and practices.

[782]

Of noble character—say the skillful [ones]—
Is a monastic at peace and fully stilled[3]
Who does not speak of one's own virtue,
Or have any arrogance anywhere in the world.

[783]

Those who see personal advantage
  In tainted doctrines[4]
  They concoct, make up and revere,
  Depend on an unstable peace.

[784]

It's not easy to overcome being entrenched in views:
  Wishing to take up a doctrine,[5]
  [Such] a person would adopt or reject
  A doctrine based on being entrenched.

[785]

Those who are cleansed do not form a view[6]
  About states of becoming or nonbecoming
    anywhere in the world.
  Having abandoned illusions and conceit,
  By what means would those who are cleansed go [to
    nonattachment]?
  They are without attachment.

[786]

One who is attached argues over doctrines—
  How and with what does one argue with someone
    unattached?
  Embracing nothing, rejecting nothing,
  Right here, a person has shaken off every view.

[787]

CHAPTER 4

The Eightfold Discourse on the Pure

Nothing to Grasp

While the preceding discourse emphasizes shaking off all views, "The Eightfold Discourse on the Pure" discourages us from grasping anything that can be seen, heard, or thought about. The likely context for this fourth discourse is an ancient Indian belief that a person acquires some of the qualities on which he or she gazes. With purity as an ultimate goal, some people believed that the purity of an object could be transferred simply through proximity. The object could be a ritual, a person, a manifestation of a god, or a meditation experience or vision of some kind. The Indian religious practice of *darśan* (literally "looking") is based on this idea of a transmission from the thing observed to the person doing the looking—or by extension, the hearing or contemplation. Closely connected to these beliefs is the idea that merit could be accumulated by contact with what was pure and that impurity could be transferred through contact with what was tainted.

This discourse rejects these views. In doing so, it redefines what it means to be a brahmin, a title traditionally reserved for the hereditary priestly class that was predominant in India at the time of the Buddha.

Traditionally, only those born into the brahmin class could be brahmins. But the *Book of Eights* uses the title *brahmin* to refer to any sage who lives according to the ethical and religious ideals outlined in the text. In a challenge to classic brahmanical practices, a true brahmin would not claim that purity is attained through "something other," such as virtue and ritual observances. In fact, according to the poem, true sages do not claim that anything will provide absolute purity, including virtue and religious observances. Because virtue and religious observances were central to brahmins' religious life, suggesting that these practices do not bring purity must have been a particularly radical critique at the time.

Overall, this discourse emphasizes that the brahmins' religious practices and beliefs were at odds with the attainment of ultimate purity, which was one of the primary goals of the brahmanical religion. The last verse takes its challenge further by boldly declaring that a (true) brahmin goes beyond (*ātiga*) boundaries (*sima*). Brahmanical life was governed by clearly defined areas of purity and by strict rules of social and ritual taboos. A brahmin who crossed the boundaries between the pure and the impure not only ignored a central practice of the religion, but went against ideas that were held as sacred. Perhaps even more radical, given the brahmanical belief in the social superiority of brahmins, the discourse ends with the claim that there is nothing to be clung to as superior.

Instead of relying on "something other," the poem advocates not clinging to anything that can be known or seen—which is to say, not clinging to anything at all. The sages who have managed this have abandoned greed. They have let go of the idea of ultimate purity. This radical nonclinging and unconcern with purity even extends to dispassion, so that, by implication, the text seems to say that complete nonclinging includes not clinging to nonclinging itself.

Suddhaṭṭhaka Sutta

The Eightfold Discourse on the Pure

[Brahmin:[1]]
"I see the Pure, the Superior, and the Healthful;
It is by what one sees that a person is purified."[2]

[The Buddha:]
"With such knowledge, having known 'the Ultimate,'
And observed 'the Pure,'
One believes in knowledge.[3]

[788]

"If people are purified by what they see,
Or if suffering is abandoned through knowledge,
Then someone with attachments[4] is purified by something other.[5]
A belief like this is betrayed by how it's proclaimed.

[789]

"No [true] brahmin speaks of purity in terms of
something other
Or in terms of virtue, [religious] observances[6]
Or what is seen, heard, or thought out.
Merit and evil do not adhere to someone
Who has left behind what's grasped,[7]
Who doesn't make up [anything] here.

[790]

"Abandoning one thing, people cling to another;
Pursuing craving, they don't transcend their clinging.
They let go, they grab;
Like a monkey, they release one branch to grasp
[another].

[791]

"People attached to concepts,[8]
In undertaking [religious] observances,
Experience[9] highs and lows.

"Great sages, having known by means of knowledge,[10]
Having understood the Dharma,
Don't experience highs and lows.

[792]

"They aren't foes to anything
Seen, heard, or thought;
How, in this world, could one have assumptions[11]
About those who see in this way, whose conduct is
open?[12]

[793]

"They don't categorize, honor,
Or claim [anything] to be 'absolute purity.'
Having abandoned[13] greed—the knot of attachment—
They do not form any wish for anything in the world.

[794]

"[True] brahmins who've crossed the boundaries[14]
Wouldn't grasp anything they can know or see in the world.
Neither passionate for passion nor obsessed by dispassion,
There is nothing here to grasp as superior.[15]"

[795]

CHAPTER 5

The Eightfold Discourse on the Ultimate

Not Relying on Anything

The major theme of "The Eightfold Discourse on the Ultimate" is the avoidance of views, which is stated most explicitly in the instruction not to "construct, prefer, or take up any doctrine." Instead, the fifth poem in the *Book of Eights* advocates such a thorough letting go that a person no longer relies on any view, including existential ideas of becoming and nonbecoming—either in this life or the next. If one isn't holding on to views, then one would never have a reason to claim that one's own doctrines are the ultimate or that someone else's are inferior. In the same way, one wouldn't think of oneself as superior, equal, or inferior to others. Any view that serves as the basis for such comparisons is called an "entanglement."

The poem places the basis or foundation for people's religious views in things that are seen, heard, or thought, as well as ideas of virtue or religious observances. Because the seen, heard, and thought are frequently listed in the Upanishads as the means for understanding truth, we can surmise that the Buddha is addressing common sources of religious knowledge prevalent at the time. "The seen" is what is seen with one's eyes and with one's inner mental vision. In the preliterate world of ancient India, where teaching and learning were done orally, "the heard" refers to what is learned from others. It's not clear whether the Pali word translated as "thought" (*muta*) refers only to what people think for themselves or whether it has a broader meaning, including any inner "knowing"—for example, what one senses or intuits. "Virtue" (*sīla*) is a broad category that may refer to the ethical qualities of a person's character, to rules of moral conduct, and to trainings one undertakes. In the context of brahmanism, "religious observances" most likely refers to rituals. However, it is possible that in the context of other religious traditions of the time, it could refer to any religious practice.

According to the poem, one shouldn't depend on any of these. If one is holding on to these, one should let go. If any of these provide knowledge, this too should be abandoned because peace is not found through knowledge. With its thorough emphasis on letting go, this discourse—as is true in most of the *Book of Eights*—advises against any religious observance or practice except letting go.

The poem refers to a person who has let go of all views as a "brahmin." Such a brahmin even lets go of the idea of social and spiritual superiority. This is ironic because brahmins considered themselves to be the highest class in society. Rather than signifying people of a particular social class whose lives centered on ideas of virtue and religious observances, here the meaning of "brahmin" is redefined as someone who is "Thus." This enigmatic title avoids categorizing people in any way, including by their religious views, hereditary class, personal qualities, or spiritual experiences. It recognizes a person as he or she appears, without definition. The poem's only positive description of a person who has thoroughly let go is as someone who is "skilled," presumably in the qualities needed to avoid clinging to anything.

Paramaṭṭhaka Sutta
The Eightfold Discourse on the Ultimate

Having views about what is "ultimate"
A person makes these the best in the world
And calls all other [views] "inferior."[1]
As such they have not gone beyond quarreling.

[796]

Seeing benefit in the Self,[2]
Or in things seen, heard, and thought
Or in precepts and religious practices,
And then grasping at this,
A person [then] sees all else as inferior.

[797]

What one relies on in order to see all else as inferior
Is an entanglement, say those who are skilled.[3]
Monastics[4] should, therefore,
Not depend on things seen, heard, or thought out
Or on virtue and [religious] observances.

[798]

Nor should they make up views in the world
By means of knowledge, precepts, and [religious] observances.

Nor would they think of themselves
Inferior or superior [to others]
And they shouldn't take themselves as equal.

[799]

Letting go of what is taken up,[5]
The person free of grasping
Doesn't depend on knowledge
Or take sides when factions disagree,
Or fall back on any kind of view.

[800]

One not inclined to either side—
to becoming or nonbecoming,
to here or the next world—
There exists nothing to get entrenched in
When considering the doctrines others grasp.

[801]

Here, one does not conceive the slightest concept[6]
In regard to what is seen, heard, or thought.
How, in this world, could one categorize the brahmin
Who does not take hold of views?

[802]

One does not construct, prefer, or take up any doctrine.[7]
A [true] brahmin not led by precepts or religious practices,
Who has gone beyond,
Does not fall back [on belief],[8]
Is one who is Thus.[9]

[803]

CHAPTER 6

The Discourse on Old Age

Free from Selfishness

"The Discourse on Old Age" is a short, pointed contemplation on death, impermanence, and loss. Life is short, the poem tells us, and only people's names continue after they die. When relatives pass away, we lose contact with them. Because the consequences of being attached to people and things are grief and despair, the sixth poem of the *Book of Eights* advises letting go of possessions and leaving behind the domestic life (*agāra*). Doing so allows one to experience peace.

The attachment emphasized here is the selfishness (*mamatta*) that leads to possessiveness, or taking things as "mine" (*mama*). Nowhere does the *Book of Eights* explicitly discuss the Buddhist teaching of "not-self," or *anatta.* In this discourse, the comparable teaching is "not-mine," or *amama.* Rather than emphasizing a doctrine or teaching about what is not-self, the focus here is on the psychological movement away from claiming things as one's own. While the nature of the self is not discussed in the *Book of Eights,* selfishness is.

As opposed to indulging in mental states like greed, despair, and selfishness, the ideal this poem points to is "seeing"—that is, directly knowing—the safety that comes from letting go of clinging. By seeing a state without possession, the sage avoids the "domestic life," a life associated with possessiveness, with taking things as "mine." Being "unattached," the sage lives in harmony, not manifesting in any state of becoming. The sage also does not view anything as being either cherished or not-cherished.

This discourse contains the simile—occurring elsewhere in the Pali *suttas*—of a drop of water not sticking to a leaf or lotus petal. The simile speaks to the way things wash off the sage—mental states like despair, envy, as well as what is seen, heard, or thought. Without any grasping, the sage is at peace even in the face of death.

Jarā Sutta
The Discourse on Old Age

Short indeed is this life—
    You will die in less than a hundred years.
    And if living longer,
    You'll die of old age.

[804]

People grieve what they take as "mine"
    —No possession exists forever.
    Having seen how it is without [possessions]
    Don't live the domestic [life].

[805]

With death, people lose
What they conceive as "mine."
Knowing this, a sage should not
Be selfishly devoted to what is "mine."

[806]

Just as, when waking up, one does not see
Someone encountered in a dream,
So one does not see loved ones
When they are dead, when their time is done.

[807]

When seen and heard
People are called by their names.
When dead,
Only the telling of their names remains.

[808]

Grief, despair, and selfishness are not abandoned
By those greedy for what is "mine."
Therefore, having abandoned grasping,
Sages live seeing safety.

[809]

A mendicant,[1] living unattached[2]
And keeping to a solitary seat,
Is said to be in harmony[3]
When not showing oneself in [any] dwelling.[4]

[810]

Independent everywhere,[5]
  Sages make nothing cherished or not-cherished;[6]
  Despair and selfishness don't stick to them
  As water doesn't stick to a leaf.

[811]

As a drop doesn't stick to a leaf
  Or water to a lotus [petal],
  So what is seen, heard, or thought
  Doesn't stick to a sage.

[812]

By being without passion and dispassion,
  Those who are cleansed[7] don't ruminate
  About what is seen, heard, or thought out,
  Nor do they wish for purity through anything else.

[813]

CHAPTER 7

The Discourse to Tissa Metteyya

Seclusion from Sex

The seventh poem in the *Book of Eights* consists of a question posed by Tissa Metteyya, followed by the Buddha's response. While we don't know who Tissa Metteyya was, it is possible he was a brahmin with the clan name of Metteyya, meaning "friend" or "friendly." A brahmin by this name is mentioned in the *Book of the Way to the Other Shore* (*Pārāyanavagga*).

A keyword in "The Discourse to Tissa Metteyya" is *viveka,* here translated as "seclusion." *Viveka* is a potent word both in the ancient Buddhist canon and in other Indian religious traditions. The importance of this concept is highlighted in the poem's statement that for noble ones, *viveka* is supreme (*uttama*). Because this discourse addresses the problems of clinging to sensual pleasures, and to sexual intercourse in particular, *viveka* could here be understood to focus on "seclusion from" or perhaps "freedom from" these pleasures. In other Buddhist texts, mental seclusion or detachment from desire and aversion is required both to enter deep meditation and to attain nirvana. In the *Chandogya Upaniṣad,* a text that predates the Buddha, *viveka* refers to the discernment or discrimination used to recognize what is most essential, meaning the Self (CU 9.6.2). In later Indian texts, the word is used to mean "liberation."

With its emphasis on avoiding sex, much of this discourse describes the dangers that can befall someone whose attachment to sex operates like a "vehicle out of control." Most of the dangers mentioned involve the judgments of others. One who indulges in sex is called "base" or "inferior" (*hīna*), loses his or her good reputation, and becomes troubled by the criticism and reprimands of others. In contrast, one is judged as being wise if he or she resolves to live the celibate, single life.

The Buddha adds that those who train in seclusion should not think of themselves as superior. Because, in ancient India, celibacy was often considered purer than noncelibacy, the temptation for renunciants to think they were better than others must have been strong. But any such conceit stands in the way of freedom.

TISSAMETTEYYA SUTTA

The Discourse to Tissa Metteyya

(Tissa Metteyya said,)[1]
"Explain, sir, the danger
For someone addicted to sex.[2]
Having heard your teaching,
We will train in seclusion."

[814]

(The Blessed One said to Metteyya,)
"For those addicted to sex
The teachings are forgotten
And the practice is mistaken.
It is something ignoble in them.

[815]

"Whoever had lived the single life
But then indulges in sex like a vehicle out of control
Is an ordinary person
Known in this world as 'base.'[3]

[816]

"Whatever praise and fame one had
Will surely waste away.
Seeing this,
One should train in giving up sex.

[817]

"Overcome by thoughts [for sex],
One burns like a wretched pauper.
In hearing disapproval from others,
One becomes [even more] troubled.

[818]

"Criticized by others
One fashions swords.
Having great greed,
One sinks into falsehoods.

[819]

"One is known as wise
When resolved on living the single life.
But when attached to sex
One is a troubled fool.

[820]

"Knowing these dangers here
A sage—both earlier and later—
Should become firm in the single life
And not indulge in sex.

[821]

"One should train in seclusion.
This, for noble ones, is supreme.
Who would not because of that think oneself
superior,
Is close to nirvana.

[822]

"People bound to sensual desires
Envy the sage living free,[4]
Who unconcerned with sensual desires,
Has crossed beyond the flood."

[823]

CHAPTER 8

The Discourse to Pasūra

Not Opposing Any Views

"The Discourse to Pasūra" provides a glimpse into the culture of debate among renunciants (*samaṇa*) in ancient India. The references to judges for these debates and to the assemblies in which they occurred suggest that the debates were organized events, not simply the informal back-and-forth that might take place in spontaneous encounters. The reference to those who seek opponents to debate suggests a combativeness and an eagerness to engage in these arguments. A Theravada commentary on this eighth discourse in the *Book of Eights* depicts Pasūra as a renunciant who wandered around actively looking for people to challenge. When he tries to engage the Buddha in debate, the Buddha responds with the teachings he gives in this chapter.

This poem emphatically depicts these debaters in unfavorable ways. They are entrenched in their views, they lust for the chance to argue, they are passionate for praise, they speak with arrogance, they become bewildered when criticized, and they despair when rejected by the judges. In these descriptions, the emphasis is on the relationship people have to their views rather than the truth or falseness of the views themselves. The discourse is concerned with how views are held, not what the views are.

The unfavorable depictions of debaters exist in sharp contrast to those who do not oppose any views. People who debate claim that only their way leads to purity, whereas the ideal person doesn't contest such claims. Rather, as we saw in Chapter 5, the ideal person doesn't cling to anything as being ultimate.

This doesn't mean the Buddha is suggesting that one should have no views. In fact, the narrator seems to advocate the view or teaching that one should avoid holding tight to any view; there is no peace in clinging.

Pasūra Sutta
The Discourse to Pasūra

They say,
    "Only here is there purity."
They say,
    "No other doctrines are pure."
    Entrenched in truths of their own,
    They call "good" whatever they depend on.

[824]

Lusting for debates and plunging into assemblies,
They take each other to be fools.
They speak relying on what others have said.
Passionate for praise, they call [themselves] skillful.

[825]

Wishing for praise while debating in an assembly,
They become anxious.
Refuted, they become depressed.
Criticized and shaken,
They seek [their opponents'] faults.

[826]

One whose doctrine is called deficient,
And by the judges, rejected,
Despairs and grieves.
The inferior debater moans, "I have been defeated."

[827]

Renunciants are elated and deflated
By the disputes that arise among them.
Seeing this, you should abstain from disputes—
They provide no benefit other than being praised.

[828]

When being praised
For proclaiming their creed in an assembly
They laugh and become conceited,
Having gotten what they wished.

[829]

While that conceit is a basis for distress,
Still they speak with arrogance and pride.
Seeing this, one shouldn't dispute—
[Disputes] don't lead to purity, say those who are skilled.

[830]

Wishing for an opponent, you roar
Like a hero nourished on royal food.
Run off, O Hero, to where the fight is;
As before, there is no fight here.

[831]

If, grasping to a view and disputing, they say,
"This alone is true,"
Tell them,
"In this dispute you have no opponent here."

[832]

Pasūra, what opponent would you get
From those who live without opponents,
Who don't counter views with views,
Who don't grasp anything here as ultimate?

[833]

And now that you've come here speculating,
Thinking out viewpoints with your own mind,
You're paired with someone cleansed
And so you can't proceed.

[834]

CHAPTER 9

The Discourse to Māgaṇḍiya

Peace without Views

Containing some of the most quoted teachings of the *Book of Eights,* this *sutta* repeats two of the anthology's major themes: the avoidance of both sensual pursuits and clinging to views. "The Discourse to Māgaṇḍiya" also contains provocative teachings that seem to deemphasize the role of virtue and religious practices in attaining the peace the Buddha claims to have attained.

The book's ninth poem takes the form of a dialogue between the Buddha and a man named Māgaṇḍiya. The discussion begins abruptly and quite dramatically as the Buddha tells Māgaṇḍiya that he avoids sex because he is familiar with craving, aversion, and lust. He then adds that he would not touch "this," which is full of urine and excrement. From Māgaṇḍiya's response, it seems "this" refers to a beautiful woman.

Surprised that the Buddha is not interested in a beautiful woman, Māgaṇḍiya then asks the Buddha about his worldview, virtue, practices, and what state of becoming he advocates. These questions refer to the four traditional areas of a person's religious life. In asking about a state of becoming, Māgaṇḍiya is most likely asking to what form of rebirth the Buddha subscribes.

The Buddha replies that he does not proclaim a doctrine (*dhammā*). Instead, through not clinging to any doctrines or views, he has experienced inner peace (*ajjhatta santi*). When Māgaṇḍiya then asks what he means by "inner peace," the Buddha doesn't answer directly. He says that those who are peaceful have no desire for states of becoming because they have let go, don't grasp, and aren't dependent on anything. In this way, the Buddha avoids talking about peace in terms of what is present, thus avoiding turning peace into a mental object one can strive for and cling to.

The emphasis on letting go and not relying on anything makes it clear that the peace the Buddha teaches is not dependent on views, learning, knowledge, virtue, or religious practices. He says that the wise don't discuss this peace in terms of the presence or absence of these factors. For those who were deeply invested in these things, the Buddha's approach must have been a radical alternative. For Māgaṇḍiya, the Buddha's statement was bewildering.[1]

His confusion may partly stem from two different meanings of the same Pali grammatical expression. It seems that Māgaṇḍiya understands the Buddha has altogether rejected views, learning, precepts, and religious practices as a means of attaining peace and purity, when in fact the Buddha is actually saying that these do not *characterize* peace. Views, learning, precepts, and religious practices could have a role along the path to peace in the same way that taking a road to the beach may be required to get to the ocean, but swimming in the ocean is not caused by taking the road.

In the last four verses, the Buddha describes some of the qualities of a sage. He may be doing so in response to a second question Māgaṇḍiya poses in verse 838 about how inner peace is manifested by someone who has it. Except for advocating peace, the Buddha only describes sages by what they don't do, reinforcing the earlier idea that a sage isn't described in terms of views, learning, virtue, or practices.

The poem's repeated reference to disputes over views suggests an environment of intellectual conflict between competing philosophers and religious practitioners. A sense of verbal conflict also pervades the poem itself, beginning when the Buddha says he avoids "this, full of urine and excrement." It continues with Māgaṇḍiya saying the Buddha's teaching is foolish, to which the Buddha responds that it is Māgaṇḍiya who is confused. This atmosphere of conflict stands in contrast to descriptions of the sage who is peaceful and doesn't quarrel with anyone. In reading the poem, it's useful to keep in mind that setting up this contrast is one of the poem's literary techniques, reinforcing the power of its message.

One of the significant teachings in this *sutta* is the importance of avoiding thinking in terms of superiority, inferiority, or equality. Not making these kinds of comparisons is a good strategy for avoiding conflict with others. This form of comparative thinking could apply to teachings and practices or to social status. Peace can be found by those who are unconcerned with the categories of superior, inferior, or equal.

Māgaṇḍiya Sutta

The Discourse to Māgaṇḍiya

[The Buddha said,]
"Seeing craving, aversion, and lust[2]
I have no desire for sex.
What is this, full of urine and excrement,
[That] I don't want to touch even with my foot?"[3]
[835]

[Māgaṇḍiya responded,]
"If you do not wish for such a jewel
As this woman desired by many kings,
What kind of worldview, virtue, practice, lifestyle,
And state of becoming do you declare?"
[836]

("Māgaṇḍiya," said the Blessed One,)
"Considering the doctrines [people] cling to,
It does not occur to me to say
'I proclaim this.'
Seeing—but not grasping—these views,[4]
I knew and saw inner peace."
[837]

(Māgaṇḍiya asked,)
"Sage, you speak without clinging
To preconceived opinions;
What is the meaning of this 'inner peace'?
How is it made known by the wise?"[5]

[838]

(The Blessed One said to Māgaṇḍiya,)
"They don't speak of purity in terms of
Views, learning, knowledge, precepts, and
[religious] observances.[6]
Nor do they speak of it in terms of the absence of
Views, learning, knowledge, precepts, or observances.
It is by letting go, not grasping, and not being
dependent
That they, the peaceful, do not hunger for becoming."

[839]

(Māgaṇḍiya said,)
"If one doesn't say purity comes through
Views, learning, knowledge, precepts, or observances,
And if one doesn't say it comes without
Views, learning, knowledge, precepts, or observances,
Then this seems to me a foolish teaching
[For] there are those who believe purity comes by
means of views."[7]

[840]

(The Blessed One said to Māgaṇḍiya,)
"Questioning based on your own views.
  And confused by your own clinging
  You don't perceive the slightest notion [of what I say].[8]
  This is why you see it as foolish.

[841]

"By thinking about equal, superior, or inferior
  One will enter in disputes.
  Unmoved by these three categories
  One won't think about 'equal' or 'superior.'[9]

[842]

"Why would [true] brahmins say, 'This is true'?
  With whom would they dispute, 'This is false'?
  Those for whom equal and not equal do not exist,
  With whom would they engage in dispute?

[843]

"Letting go of home,
  Wandering without a household,
  Not becoming intimate with villagers
  Free from sensual desire,
  Free of expectations,
  A sage won't quarrel with people.[10]

[844]

"Whatever one should live detached from,
The mighty one[11] neither grasps nor disputes.
Just as a lotus grows in water
Unsullied by water and mud,
So a sage without greed, who advocates peace,
Is unsullied by sensuality and the world.

[845]

"Those who know don't become proud[12]
In regard to views or what is thought out.
They are not influenced by action or by learning;
They don't end up entrenched.

[846]

"Someone freed from concepts has no ties,[13]
Someone freed by wisdom has no delusions.
Those who grasp at concepts and views
Clash as they walk through the world."

[847]

CHAPTER 10

The Discourse on Before Breaking Apart

Peaceful and Independent

The subject of this poem is peace. "The Discourse on Before Breaking Apart" begins with a question asking what a person sees and how a person behaves when he or she is peaceful. In the subsequent verses, the Buddha addresses the second part of the question—how such a person behaves. It could be that the Buddha intentionally ignores the issue of what a peaceful person sees because being at peace doesn't depend on seeing anything. It doesn't depend on anything at all.

Throughout this tenth poem (and much of the *Book of Eights*) the Buddha primarily describes peaceful people not by what they do, but what they don't do. They don't crave or cling to anything. They aren't angry, fearful, or greedy. They're not concerned with sensual pleasures. They're not attached to doctrines or views. They have no possessions, and they aren't dependent on anything. All these characterizations suggest that being peaceful doesn't rely on doing or having anything in particular.

Instead, peace is present when craving or clinging is absent. This depiction of peace doesn't rely on doctrines, beliefs, attainments, or metaphysical realms. The emphasis on what *not* to do undermines any attachment to what one thinks one should do.

The Buddha doesn't mention anything here about letting go or abandoning attachments. That's because letting go is only relevant if one is clinging to something; abandoning is only needed if one has mental impulses that bring suffering. These actions aren't needed by a person who has attained the kind of peace the Buddha is championing.

As noted in the previous chapter, the Buddha's descriptions of a sage were most likely provocative in ancient India. Among people who espoused various doctrines, the claim that sages aren't guided by views must have seemed peculiar. To people who put great value on wealth and children, the idea that a sage is someone who has no possessions and no children might have been disconcerting. For those who venerated gods, priests, and sacred things, it might have seemed irreverent for sages not to revere anything.

Compounding this irreverence, the Buddha describes sages as faithless. But this is a form of wordplay. Sages are faithless because after becoming peaceful, they no longer need faith. Similar wordplay is perhaps present in the statement that sages don't free themselves from passion. Those who considered passion a primary hindrance to overcome probably had trouble with the idea that sages don't free themselves from its entanglements. However, the reason sages don't free themselves from passion is because they've already done so; this freedom is one of the defining characteristics of a sage.

In a few instances, the discourse specifies particular behavior and qualities attributed to an ideal person. In addition to being at peace, such a person is described as teaching without pride and as being gentle, intelligent, equanimous, and mindful. They are also not dependent on anything, "having understood the Dharma." Furthermore, they teach without agitation.

In verse 849, the person at peace is described as being free of craving before he or she dies. The attainment of peace was clearly understood as something one could attain before dying, or breaking apart.[1]

Purābheda Sutta

The Discourse on Before Breaking Apart

[Questioner:]
"Seeing what and behaving how[2]
Is one said to be 'at peace'?
Tell about this, Gotama, when you are asked
About supreme people."

[848]

(The Blessed One said,)
"Free of craving before [their] death,[3]
Independent of past and future,
Not making up anything in the present,
They revere nothing.

[849]

"Free of anger, free of fear,
Not boasting, not worrying,
They are sages who, when speaking,
Teach[4] without agitation.

[850]

"Not clinging to the future,
Nor grieving the past,
They see seclusion in the midst of sense contacts
And are not guided by views.

[851]

"They are neither clinging[5] nor deceitful,
Not greedy or stingy,
Neither impudent nor offensive,
And don't engage in malicious speech.

[852]

"Neither addicted to what's pleasant,
Nor given to arrogance,
Gentle and intelligent,
They are faithless and don't free themselves from passion.[6]

[853]

"Not training for the love of possessions,
They're not upset with a lack of possessions.
They are not hindered by cravings
And don't covet tasty [foods].

[854]

"Always equanimous and mindful,
In this world they don't think of themselves as
Equal, superior, or inferior.
They have no swollen pride.

[855]

"Depending on nothing;
Having known the Dharma, they are independent.
They have no craving
For becoming and not-becoming.

[856]

"I say they are at peace;
They who are not concerned with sensual pleasures;
They have no bonds
And have crossed beyond attachments.

[857]

"They have no children,
Cattle, fields,
Or possessions;
There's nothing they take up or discard.[7]

[858]

"Not revering what
Commoners, renunciants, and brahmins
Say about them,
They are not agitated by [any] talk.[8]

[859]

"Neither greedy nor selfish, sages don't claim to be
Superior, equal, or inferior;
Being free of comparisons,
They do not compare.[9]

[860]

"Taking nothing in the world as their own,
Having no sorrow for what doesn't exist,
And uninvolved in doctrines
They are called 'peaceful.'"

[861]

CHAPTER 11

The Discourse on Quarrels and Disputes

Understanding Conditionality

This important discourse presents the Buddha as someone who knows a path of knowledge. From the poem's perspective, this path is one of practical insight into the basis of quarrels, sorrow, selfishness, and conceit. The key insight refers to understanding conditionality—that is, how things depend on the presence of preexisting conditions. "The Discourse on Quarrels and Disputes" specifically mentions the conditional nature of experiences people take to be the highest spiritual attainments. Because they are conditional, the attainments cannot be ultimate, and if they are not ultimate, they cannot serve as a reliable basis for debates and conceits about one's religious beliefs and attainments. After understanding these attainments as conditional, one will no longer get involved in disputes about them.

This poem, the eleventh in the *Book of Eights,* is organized as a series of questions and answers. Traditionally it's assumed that the person answering the questions is the Buddha. The one asking the questions most likely represents someone familiar with the Upanishads who can understand the Buddha's wordplay in the last verse. Here, referring to the teachings of others, the Buddha uses a phrase that can mean either "knowing these claims are conditional" or "knowing these claims are [related to the] Upanishad." This wordplay was probably a verbal challenge to the supremacy the Upanishads' teachings—possibly that of *The Upanishad of the Great Forest* (*Bṛhadāraṇyaka Upaniṣad*), a text that represented some of the religious teachings current in India at the time of the Buddha.

The teachings in the *Bṛhadāraṇyaka Upaniṣad* provide a helpful context for understanding the "Discourse on Quarrels and Disputes." If the questioner is a follower of the Upanishads, then the *Bṛhadāraṇyaka Upaniṣad* clarifies what he is asking and why. This text can also help us understand what the Buddha is responding to. The Buddha is not using the occasion to explain his full approach to religious life. Rather, he is offering his perspective in response to the particular concerns of the questioner.

"The Discourse on Quarrels and Disputes" begins with the question "From where come quarrels, disputes, despair, and sorrow, as well as selfishness, pride, conceit, and malicious speech?" In asking "from where," the questioner wants to know the underlying foundation or precondition from which human conflict and self-centeredness arise. Asking "where" echoes questions in the *Bṛhadāraṇyaka Upaniṣad* that ask where things are established or supported. Both the *Bṛhadāraṇyaka Upaniṣad* and "The

Discourse on Quarrels and Disputes" share the technique of using a series of "where" questions to go deeper and deeper in an attempt to reach the foundations on which things ultimately rely. In the case of the *Bṛhadāraṇyaka Upaniṣad* (3.9.19–26), the series of questions and answers ends with a statement regarding an essence claimed to exist within all people—the *ātman,* or the eternal Self/ Soul.

By contrast, in the "Discourse on Quarrels and Disputes," the Buddha explains that quarrels, disputes, despair, and sorrow, as well as selfishness, pride, conceit, and malicious speech, have "what is cherished" as their foundation. The questioner then asks where the basis is for what is cherished. The answer: desire.

In further questions and answers, a progressively deeper series of underlying foundations is described. Desire is dependent on pleasantness and unpleasantness. The foundation for pleasantness and unpleasantness is sense contact—the seeing, hearing, smelling, touching, and tasting experienced when the senses are stimulated. Sense contact depends on the presence of the names and appearances of the objects perceived. The Buddha then adds, "With the disappearance of appearances, sense contact doesn't occur." In other words, if whatever can be seen, heard, smelled, touched, or tasted disappears, the senses will not be stimulated.

Up to this point in the poem, the foundations exist in relationship to each other in the following order (listed in reverse from how they appear in the poem):

> Name and appearances are the foundation for contact.
>
> Contact is the foundation for pleasantness and unpleasantness.
>
> Pleasantness and unpleasantness are the foundation for desire.
>
> Desire is the foundation for what is cherished.
>
> What is cherished is the foundation for quarrels and so on.

After the Buddha explains that "name and appearance" (*nāma rūpa*) is the foundation for sense contact, he goes on to say, "With the disappearance of appearances, contact doesn't occur." The interrogator takes a keen interest in the idea of "disappearance," asking, "Associated with what do appearances disappear?" The teachings of the *Bṛhadāraṇyaka Upaniṣad* are helpful in understanding why the questioner asks a "how" question rather than another "where" question.

In one of the creation myths described in the *Bṛhadāraṇyaka Upaniṣad* (1.4.7), the original undif-ferentiated universe was first distinguished through names and appearances—by what things were called and how they physically looked. In other words, the foundation for everything that can be perceived in the world is the separation of things into their names and appearance. The only thing prior to or more basic than name and appearance is the undifferentiated universe, about which nothing can be said. This means that it would not occur to someone familiar with this creation myth to ask where the basis is for name and appearance.

Outside of its creation myth, the *Bṛhadāraṇyaka Upan-*

iṣad also uses *nāma* as a synonym for the *ātman*—the eternal Self/Soul of each person. With this meaning, the differentiation of the universe into names and appearances refers to a distinction between the core Self and everything else.

The *Bṛhadāraṇyaka Upaniṣad* explains that a person's physical appearance disappears when he or she dies, when the body disintegrates after death. However, a person's *nāma*—here synonymous with the *ātman*—is infinite and will never disappear. By recognizing the eternal nature of one's *nāma/ātman,* one attains the ultimate realization championed by the *Bṛhadāraṇyaka Upaniṣad* (3.2.12). The infinity of the *nāma* is probably referring to the teaching in the Upanishads that the *ātman* pervades the entire universe. When one fully realizes one's *ātman,* the *ātman* and the universe are known to be the same. The corollary to this is that the distinction between the *ātman* and everything else is ultimately false. All appearances would also ultimately be unreal.

The most likely reason the questioner asks how appearances disappear is that the questioner believes in the idea represented by the *Bṛhadāraṇyaka Upaniṣad* that when one realizes the *ātman,* all appearances disappear. Thus the disappearance of appearances is a desirable outcome. The obvious question then is how appearances can disappear.

The Buddha responds with the following verse:

Appearances disappear when
  Not conceiving concepts,
  Not conceiving false concepts,

Not nonconceiving,
And not conceiving disappearance.
This is because conceiving is the basis of conceptual
differentiation.

(verse 874)

For the Buddha, appearances arise together with conceptualization. Stated differently, distinguishing one appearance from everything else arises together with our naming (*nāma*) of the appearance. Based on this idea, the first part of the answer is straightforward: appearances disappear when concepts aren't created. Appearances also disappear when there are no false concepts. The idea seems to be that erroneous concepts can contribute to appearances, an idea that the *Bṛhadāraṇyaka Upaniṣad* implies is involved when people lose touch with the undifferentiated oneness of *ātman* and the universe. The Buddha also says that the disappearance of appearances does not involve a state of nonconceiving. This may mean that while no conceiving actually occurs, the mind retains the capacity to conceive, remaining conscious and alert. Lastly, holding on to concepts of disappearance doesn't lead to the disappearance of appearances; the concept of an event is different from the event itself, and the idea of something disappearing is not the same as its actual disappearance.

It's possible that in his answer the Buddha is describing a particular state of meditation where ordinary perception and conceptualization cease. Whether or not this is a meditative state, the questioner is satisfied with the answer, probably because it resembles familiar Upanishadic teachings on the undifferentiated consciousness that is attained when the *ātman* is realized as ultimate reality. In the *Bṛhadāraṇyaka Upaniṣad* (4.3.30), when one realizes the Self, nothing in the world that is separate from the Self can be the object of perception. In this state, the Self remains conscious, but it will not actually perceive or conceive anything because for perception or conception to occur, there has to be a differentiation between the perceiver and the perceived.

To find out if the Buddha considers this (meditative) state the ultimate attainment, the interrogator asks if the "highest purity of spirit goes only this far?" The term *spirit* (*yakkha*) is probably an honorific way of referring to a respected spiritual practitioner—in this case, the Buddha. In reply, the Buddha explains two different attainments that some people hold as the highest. The first is the (meditative) state described in verse 874. This is an attainment that can be reached while one is still alive. The second attainment occurs when there is "no residue of grasping." This refers to the idea that complete freedom is not attained until death; as long as one is alive, having a body is the residue of past grasping.

The Buddha neither agrees nor disagrees with these claims to the highest form of purity. If he did, he would be entering into a dispute over rival assertions. Instead he says that these claims are conditional and that sages study the conditional nature of things. The implication is that these are not ultimate. The poem ends with the statement that a liberated person who knows does not associate with becoming or nonbecoming. In relation to the teachings in the *Bṛhadāraṇyaka Upaniṣad,* this may mean that someone who is liberated is unconcerned with whether or not the Self continues after death.

It is noteworthy that in "The Discourse on Quarrels and Disputes," the Buddha does not specifically teach letting go of disputes. This may be because he's describing someone who is already free, someone who has let go and has no interest in grasping again.

Kalahavivāda Sutta

The Discourse on Quarrels and Disputes

[Questioner:]
"From where come
Quarrels, disputes, despair, and sorrow,
As well as selfishness, pride,
Conceit, and malicious speech?
From where have they come? Answer us, please."

[862]

[Buddha:]
"From what is cherished[1]
Come quarrels, disputes, despair, and sorrow,
As well as selfishness, pride,
Conceit, and malicious speech.
Quarrels and disputes are tied to selfishness.
Maligning others arises with disputes."

[863]

[Questioner:]
"Where is the foundation for what is cherished in the world
And for the greed that operates in the world?
Where is the basis for the hopes and aims
People have for a future [state]?"[2]

[864]

[Buddha:]
"Desires[3] are the foundation for what is cherished in the world
And for the greed that operates in the world.
This is the basis for the hopes and aims
People have for a future [state]."

[865]

[Questioner:]
"Where is the foundation for desire in the world?[4]
And from where have arisen
Judgments, anger, lies, uncertainty,
And the mental qualities spoken of by the Renunciant?"[5]

[866]

[Buddha:]
"Desire arises dependent on the pair
This world calls 'agreeable' and 'disagreeable.'[6]
Seeing the becoming and nonbecoming of appearances[7]
A person creates judgments in this world.

[867]

"When these pairs exist, so do
The states of anger, lies, and uncertainty.
Whoever is uncertain should train in the way of knowledge,[8]
For it is from having known that the Renunciant spoke of mental states."

[868]

[Questioner:]
"Where is the foundation for what is agreeable and disagreeable?
What must not exist for these not to occur?
Tell me where is the origin for whatever is meant by
'Becoming' and 'not-becoming.'"

[869]

[Buddha:]
"[Sense] contact is the foundation for pleasantness and unpleasantness;
With the nonexistence of contact these don't occur.
This is the basis for whatever is meant by
'Becoming' and 'not-becoming.'"

[870]

[Questioner:]
"Where is the foundation for contact in this world?
From where does grasping arise?[9]
With the nonexistence of what does selfishness not occur?
With the nonbecoming of what does contact not occur?"

[871]

[Buddha:]
"Contact is dependent on name and appearance.[10]
Longing is the basis of grasping.
When longing doesn't exist, selfishness doesn't occur.
With the disappearance of appearances, contact doesn't occur."

[872]

[Questioner:]
"Associated with what do appearances disappear?
How do pleasure and pain disappear?
Tell me this;
I am motivated to know how they disappear."

[873]

[Buddha:]
"Appearances disappear when
Not conceiving concepts,[11]
Not conceiving false concepts,[12]
Not nonconceiving,
And not conceiving disappearance.
This is because conceiving is the basis of conceptual differentiation.[13]"

[874]

[Questioner:]
"You've explained what we have asked.
We ask another question. Please answer [it].
Do learned ones here say highest purity of the spirit[14] goes only this far?
Or do they say it is something more than this?"

[875]

[Buddha:]
"Some learned ones say
The highest purity of spirit goes only this far.
But some who claim to be experts explain it [occurs] at the time
When there is no residue of grasping.[15]

[876]

"Knowing, '[both] these [claims] are conditional,'[16]
A sage investigates conditionality.
Knowing, the liberated one doesn't get into disputes.
This wise one doesn't associate[17] with
Becoming or not-becoming."

[877]

CHAPTER 12

The Shorter Discourse on the Dead End

Living without Conflict

In "The Shorter Discourse on the Dead End,"[1] the Buddha makes an astonishing revelation: he does not claim anything to be "the truth." This was undoubtedly a surprising thing to assert, given the context of religious debates and competing claims of truth. The declaration can be seen as one of the distinguishing characteristics of the Buddha's teachings. It also raises the question, if the Buddha does not teach the truth, what does he teach?

In accord with not teaching "the truth," in this twelfth poem the Buddha offers no religious doctrine or teachings of his own. When he is asked whose claims are true among those quarreling about the truth, the Buddha avoids answering the question. Instead he responds by explaining that people "make their very own view to be true." In other words, the people who argue are not debating the truth, they are quarreling over what they have constructed as true.

Instead of arbitrating whose religious claims are true, the Buddha comments on the absurdity of how some people argue about the truth. Everyone would be equally a fool if the only criterion for being a fool is not approving an opponent's doctrine. On the other hand, no one would be a fool if one is wise merely because one claims to be. These contradictory conclusions are, of course, untenable. In these comments, the Buddha is not saying anything about the truth or falsehood of the people's truth claims. Rather he is pointing to the inadequacy of some of the (simplistic) ways people argue that they are right and others are wrong.

The Buddha is then asked, "Why don't renunciants say one [and the same thing]?" He answers,

> There is only one truth;
> There exists no other [truth] by which a person can dispute with others.
> Because [in this way]they proclaim their own different truths,
> Renunciants do not say one [and the same thing].
>
> (verse 884)

This is the only occurrence in the entire Pali canon where the Buddha says there is only one truth. This statement is unlikely to represent the Buddha's own position on truth, especially because it so clearly contradicts his claim earlier in the poem that he doesn't speak of anything as the truth. If he taught that there is only one truth, he would then stand in opposition to the "made-up" truths of others. He would also be contradicting one of the central themes of the *Book of Eights*—that of avoiding claiming or debating any doctrines, views, or ideas as being the ultimate.

Most likely "There is only one truth" is a rhetorical statement expressing the viewpoint of those who assert their own claims of truth.[2] In other words, the Buddha answers the question of why renunciants don't all say the same thing by explaining the logic that prevents them from agreeing. In doctrinal quarrels, it is common to assume one's own doctrine is true to the exclusion of all others. Debates over religious teachings seldom allow for the possibility of more than one truth. A debate over which claim is true would be nonsensical if both were equally true. Therefore, the stance taken by those who debate such matters is, "There is only one truth; there exists no other [truth] by which a person can quarrel with others."

The Buddha is therefore not asserting that there is only one truth. That this is the case is further supported by the explanation that

> Except for concepts,[3] there are not
> Many, varied and constant truths in the world.
>
> (verse 886)

In other words, the varied truths that renunciants proclaim are all ideas conceptualized in the mind. There are no natural, self-contained truths—only ideas that people have created and adopted. This is similar to the teaching in the preceding chapter, "The Discourse on Quarrels and Disputes," in that quarrels and disputes have their origin in concepts and conceptual abstractions, thus reinforcing the instruction to be wary of concepts.

Rather than championing a religious truth, the Buddha focuses on how one gets into conflict and how one avoids it. Because he understands this, he confidently declares, "Those who've abandoned all judgments create no conflict in the world." With his radical avoidance of all truth claims, the only thing the Buddha offers in this discourse is the possibility of living without conflict.

Cūḷabyūha Sutta

The Shorter Discourse of the Dead End

[Questioner:]
"Each abiding in their own views,
The many experts quarrel, claiming,
'Knowing this, one understands the Dharma.
Rejecting it, one is imperfect.'[4]

[878]

"Quarreling, they argue,
'My opponent is unskilled and a fool!'
As they are each called 'experts,'
Which of their claims is true?"

[879]

[The Buddha:]
"If, by not approving an opponent's doctrine[5]
One becomes a fool, an animal of deficient wisdom,
Then all who are stuck in their views
Are fools, are of deficient wisdom.

[880]

"And if they are all cleansed by their views
And if they all have pure wisdom, skill, and intelligence,
Then no one would have deficient wisdom.
All would be equal with regard to their views.

[881]

"I do not say, 'This is the truth,'[6]
Which is what fools say in contradicting each other.
They make their very own view to be true
And so claim their opponent to be a fool."

[882]

[Questioner:]
"What some say is the truth,
Others say is empty and false.
Arguing like this, they quarrel.
Why don't renunciants say one [and the same thing]?"

[883]

[The Buddha:]
"'There is only one truth;
There exists no other [truth] by which a person can
dispute with others.'
Because [in this way] they proclaim their own
different truths,
Renunciants do not say one [and the same thing]."

[884]

[Questioner:]
"Why do those who argue, who say that they are
skilled,
Speak a variety of truths?
Have they learned many and varied truths
Or is it speculation that they follow?"

[885]

[The Buddha:]
"Except for concepts,[7] there are not
Many, varied and constant truths in the world.
Having worked out the logic of [their] views
They say there are two things: the true and the false.

[886]

"Based on what is seen, heard, and thought out,
And on precepts and religious practices, they show
contempt.
Taking a stand in what they have determined,
And happy with themselves
They say 'My opponent is foolish and unskilled.'

[887]

"They call themselves skilled
Based on how they call their opponents fools.
In claiming themselves skilled,
They disrespect others who make the same claim
[for themselves].

[888]

"'Perfect' according to unwarranted views
Drunk with conceit, thinking they're complete,
They, by their own selves, consecrate their minds
And equally so their views.

[889]

"If one is deficient because opponents [say so]
Then one's opponents would be deficient as well.
But if, because one says so oneself, one is knowing and wise,
Then, among the renunciants, no one is a fool.

[890]

"Because they are aroused with passion for their views,
Sectarians say in myriad ways,
'They who preach a doctrine other than ours
Have failed in purity, they are unaccomplished.'

[891]

"'Purity is only here,' they claim.
'Purity is not in any other Dharma,' they say.
Entrenched like this in many ways,
Sectarians speak firmly about their own path.

[892]

"Adamant about their own path
What opponent here would they claim is a fool?
If they called their opponent a fool with an impure doctrine,
They would only bring strife on themselves.

[893]

"Set in what they've decided,
Having themselves as the standard,[8]
They get into quarrels in this world.
But those who've abandoned all judgments
Create no conflict in the world."

[894]

CHAPTER 13

The Greater Discourse of the Dead End

Peace Instead of Doctrine

The overarching theme of "The Greater Discourse of the Dead End" is the futility and absurdity of intense debates and disputes about religious and philosophical doctrines. If the title of the thirteenth discourse in the *Book of Eights* reflects this main theme, then these debates can be seen as "dead ends," leading nowhere.[1] The Buddha unequivocally asserts that sages do not get involved in doctrines—not even to oppose them. Without opposing any particular doctrines, the Buddha criticizes the various ways that people are attached to them. He describes the problems that come with holding on to views, and he seems to assume that by understanding the problems associated with these attachments, one won't get attached. Instead one will focus on peace, a peace that doesn't need a doctrine.

As he highlights the problems that come with attachment to views, the Buddha describes a number of consequences of championing them. People who seek praise for successfully arguing for their preferred view discover that obtaining praise doesn't bring tranquility. Those who are entrenched in their views aren't easily trained in the path of peace. Holding views that emphasize the importance of purity can bring great distress when one's purity is compromised. Furthermore, if a doctrine is deemed inferior simply because it is receives criticism, no doctrine could be considered superior—or even adequate—since all doctrines are bound to be criticized. Using a similar logic, if a doctrine is deemed true simply because people worship it, then because people revere their own religious doctrines, all religious doctrines would be true.

As we've seen in other discourses, people who avoid attachments to views are called sages. Such sages—twice referred to as brahmins in this poem—are described in social, doctrinal, and personal terms. Socially, sages are peaceful among those not at peace. They are not led by others and do not follow any faction involved in a dispute. Doctrinally, sages neither argue the validity of any doctrine (*dhammā*) nor hold up any doctrine as superior. They know safety is found in the absence of disputes. On a personal level, sages have equanimity and have laid down their burden—that is, the attachments they once held. They are released from significant attachments that the poem calls "old contaminants" (*pubba āsava*). Presumably these are old because they accompany a person for a long time before they're relinquished. The *Book of Eights* does not explain what these contaminants are. In other early Buddhist literature, they are listed as sensual craving, becoming, and ignorance.

By emphasizing letting go of all virtuous conduct and religious observances, all blamable and blameless actions, and having no desire for purity or impurity, this discourse offers a radical alternative to some of the religious ideals of ancient India, especially those of the traditional brahmins. The alternative is nonclinging. True brahmins cling to nothing whatsoever, not even peace.

The radical nature of this poem raises many questions. In letting go of blamable and blameless actions, as well as the desire for purity and impurity, and not clinging to peace, how does a sage live? Does a sage avoid being virtuous or doing things that are blameless? Is this an ideal of ethical indifference and inaction? The discourse itself does not answer many of the questions its radical message calls forth. From the perspective of the poem, perhaps such questions don't need to be answered, only abandoned.

Mahābyūha Sutta
The Greater Discourse of the Dead End

[The Buddha:]
"Abiding in their own views,
All who argue, 'This alone is true'
Either incur blame
Or obtain praise.

[895]

"[Praise] is a trifle, not enough to bring tranquility.
I say [praise and blame] are the two fruits of disputes;
Having observed this, one shouldn't dispute,
Seeing safety is the place without disputes.

[896]

"One who knows doesn't get involved
In any particular opinion.[2]
Why would someone who is unattached,
Who doesn't go along with what's seen and heard, become attached?[3]

[897]

"Those who say virtue is ultimate
Dedicate themselves to purity and religious observances.[4]
[Saying], 'Only by training in this will there be purity.'
Claiming to be skillful, they are faced with [further] becoming.

[898]

"One who falls away from virtue and observances
Trembles at having failed at the task,
And hopes for—longs for—purity,
As a poor, far-off traveler [hopes for—longs for—home].[5]

[899]

"But whoever
Has let go of all virtuous conduct and observances,
As well as all actions blamable and blameless,
And who has no wishes for 'purity' or 'impurity,'
Lives without indulging, not [even] taking up
peace.[6]

[900]

"[Whoever] depends on austerities,
And on what is seen, heard, and thought,
Wails for purity,
Not free from craving for becoming and not
becoming.

[901]

"Longing comes from wanting,
And with planning there is fear.
But with no death and rebirth here,
How could one fear, what could one long for?"

[902]

[Questioner:]
"That doctrine some say is the best,
Others say is inferior.
As they all claim to be experts,
Which statement is true?"

[903]

[The Buddha replied,]
"They say their own doctrine is perfect.
They say the doctrine of others is inferior.
Quarreling so, they dispute;
Everyone saying their own opinion is true.

[904]

"If it is inferior because of someone's contempt
Then no doctrine would be the best.
This is because many say the doctrine of others is inferior
While advocating their own.

[905]

"If [any] 'doctrine' [people] worship is true,
As is the path they praise,
Then all doctrines would be true
And purity would belong to them all.

[906]

"[True] brahmins are not led by others
When considering doctrines believed.
They have therefore gone beyond disputes.
Indeed, they see none of these doctrines as the best.

[907]

"'I know. I see. It's just like this.'
—Some believe purity comes through views.
But if they see, what [good] is that for them?
Going too far, they say purity comes from
something other.

[908]

"Seeing, a person sees [only] names and appearances;
Having seen one knows only these.
Whether one sees much or little,
This doesn't bring purity, say the skilled.

[909]

"They who are entrenched in teachings,
Who revere preconceived views, are not easy to
train.
Whatever they depend on they say
Is beautiful, is purity, is where they see truth.[7]

[910]

"[In using] words,[8]
[True] brahmins don't make things up,
Follow views,
Or bind themselves to knowledge.
Knowing the many commonplace opinions
They are equanimous, thinking, 'That is what others
hold on to.'

[911]

"Free of worldly ties, sages here
Don't follow any faction in a dispute.
Peaceful among those not at peace,
Equanimous, thinking, 'That is what others hold on to,'
They don't hold on to [anything].

[912]

"Having given up old contaminants[9] without forming
new ones,
They neither pursue desires nor get entrenched in
doctrines.
Free from viewpoints, not clinging to the world,
Wise ones have no self-reproach.

[913]

"They are not an enemy to any doctrine
Seen, heard, or thought out.
Not forming opinions, not shut down, and not
desirous,[10]
They are sages, wise ones who have laid their burden
down.[11]"

[914]

CHAPTER 14

The Discourse on Being Quick

Release Is Peace

With this discourse, the *Book of Eights* changes significantly from the teachings and tone of the earlier discourses in the collection. Rather than criticizing clinging to views or describing the ideal sage who is at peace, "The Discourse on Being Quick" discusses how monastics should train. The emphasis on monastics is seen in the nine occurrences of the word *bhikkhu,* or "monastic," in this single poem compared to only two occurrences in all the previous discourses put together. The book's fourteenth poem also refers to the code of monastic discipline (*pātimokkha*).

Perhaps because the teachings are meant for the monastic followers of the Buddha, this discourse includes a degree of reverence and respect for the Buddha not seen in earlier chapters. Here the Buddha is given the titles Kinsman of the Sun, Unconquered Conqueror, Eyewitness to the Dharma, and the Blessed One. None of the verses in the earlier discourses mentions these designations. Instead, in the earlier chapters, the Buddha is referred to as "sir" once, and by his family name (Gotama) once.

The monastic training described in this chapter—

essentially a long list of behaviors that should be avoided—is concerned primarily with ethics. Except for one mention of being mindful, there are no references to specific religious practices or meditation techniques that monastics should perform. This is consistent with the strong emphasis in earlier chapters on letting go. Freedom isn't found through *doing* anything; it's found by not clinging. Avoiding behaviors that arise from clinging is the path to the end of clinging. With this in mind, monastics should "know release is peace" and in knowing this, train in the Buddha's message.

The Buddha's first teachings in this poem are particularly important. Here he emphasizes the destruction of the root source for conceptual proliferation which he describes as being either the idea "I am the thinker" or the thought "I am." While the grammar of the Pali phrase allows for both translations into English, the two options both identify some form of conceit as the basis from which a problematic differentiation of concepts with which the world is categorized arises. When this conceit is uprooted, the conceptual proliferation stops. A sage does not categorize or conceptualize the world with any fixed reference point of existing as "I."

While training to become such a sage, a monastic should avoid swelling up with conceit, which is described as thinking they are better, worse, or equal to others. The alternative to such comparative thinking is to have a mind that is still and unmoving like a calm sea. Many of the training instructions the Buddha mentions can be understood as support for having a still, peaceful mind.

Tuvaṭaka Sutta
The Discourse on [Being] Quick

[Questioner:]
"I ask you, O Kinsman of the Sun, Great Seer,
About seclusion and the state of peace:
By seeing what is a monastic freed,[1]
Not clinging to anything in this world?"

[915]

(The Buddha said,)
"Let them completely destroy the root
Of conceptual differentiation,[2]
That is, [the idea] 'I am the thinker.'
Ever mindful, they train to subdue their cravings.

[916]

"They shouldn't get entrenched in any teachings they know
Whether their own or that of others.
Good people say that
Being entrenched is not release.[3]

[917]

"They would not, because of this, think themselves
Better, worse, or equal [to others].
Experiencing many things,[4]
They don't take a stand in thoughts of themselves.

[918]

"Tranquil within,
A monastic wouldn't seek peace from others.
For one tranquil within,
There is nothing embraced
And so how [could anything be] rejected?[5]

[919]

"Just as when no waves appear
In the middle of a still sea,
So a monastic, still and unmoving,
Would not swell with conceit anywhere."

[920]

[Questioner:]
"The one with open eyes, the Eyewitness to the Dharma,
Proclaims the removal of danger.
Tell us, sir,
The practice, the discipline, and meditation."[6]

[921]

[The Buddha:]
"One should
Shut one's ears to village talk,
Not be covetous with one's eyes,
Not be greedy for tasty things,
Or not take anything in the world as 'mine.'

[922]

"Touched by sense experience,[7] a monastic shouldn't
  Despair about anything,
  Wish for states of becoming,
  Or tremble at terrors.

[923]

"One shouldn't hoard
  Food, drinks, and clothes received[8]
  And shouldn't fret
  When none of that's obtained.

[924]

"Meditating, not loitering around,
  Restraining restlessness,
  One shouldn't be negligent.
  A monastic should live in quiet dwellings.

[925]

"One shouldn't sleep too much.
  Ardent, one would be devoted to wakefulness.
  One should renounce laziness, deception, gaiety,
  Games, sexual intercourse, and what accompany these.

[926]

"One shouldn't practice Vedic spells or magic,[9]
  Nor interpret dreams, signs,
  The stars or [animal] sounds.
  My [disciples] should not be devoted to practicing medicine or curing infertility.

[927]

"Monastics should not be troubled by blame
Or inflated by praise.
They should dispel greed,
As well as selfishness, anger, and divisive speech.

[928]

"Monastics shouldn't be involved in buying and selling,
Or in reviling others anywhere.
They shouldn't be ill-tempered in the midst of a village,
Or talk to others with the desire for gain.

[929]

"Monastics shouldn't boast
Or speak with wrong intent.
They shouldn't train in impudence
Or talk in quarrelsome ways.

[930]

"They shouldn't be driven to lie,
Or knowingly deceive.
Nor should they disdain others
For their precepts, practices, wisdom, or way of life.

[931]

"If annoyed hearing the words
Of renunciants and ordinary folk,
They shouldn't reply harshly;
Those who retaliate are not peaceful."

[932]

[Questioner:][10]
"Knowing this Dharma, inquiring monastics,
Always mindful, would train [in it].
Knowing release[11] is peace,
They wouldn't neglect Gotama's message.

[933]

"He is the Unconquered Conqueror,
Eyewitness to the Dharma
Who saw without relying on hearsay.
With vigilance and reverence
One should train in that message of the Blessed
One."

[934]

CHAPTER 15

The Discourse on Being Violent

Training in Peace

The first five verses of "The Discourse on Being Violent" express the emotional unrest the Buddha experienced prior to his awakening. Here, we find his powerful statement of seeing impermanence: how nothing has a core and everything is changing. In a unique passage in the Pali canon, the Buddha reports how he was dismayed, shaken, and afraid at the violence and conflict he witnessed among the people of his time. He describes them as writhing about in their suffering like fish thrashing about in a puddle of water. He also saw an arrow embedded in people's hearts—including his own—that was the root of the turmoil. More importantly, he discovered that the arrow could be removed and the turmoil quelled.

In this unique, metaphorical description of his awakening, the Buddha not only saw that he could remove his own arrow, but he understood that it was possible for others to do so. Just as the turmoil he witnessed wasn't unique to him but was experienced by everyone, he understood that the solution applied to everyone as well.

The Buddha's discussion weaves back and forth between talking about himself and talking about others as if he sees no sharp separation between them.

After the first five verses, the remaining fifteen describe the training for those who want to be at peace and presumably pull out the arrow that is causing so much suffering. The sharp transition from the early autobiographical verses and the remainder of the poem is marked by the inclusion of an ancient editor's instruction that the last fifteen verses should be recited, most likely as part of communal recitations by the Buddhist monastics. The instruction to recite this section of the poem suggests that this was an important discourse in the ancient Buddhist communities.

In addition to training for peace, the training is also for attaining *nibbāna* (nirvana). I have translated *nibbāna,* a verbal noun, as "full release," partly to continue the *Book of Eights*' emphasis on letting go and partly to avoid later Buddhist ideas of *nibbāna* as a transcendent reality. In addition, translating it as "full release" reinforces the idea that "release is peace."

The training prescribed in "The Discourse on Being Violent" consists almost entirely of activities to be avoided. The only training mentioned that should be taken up is the practice of being truthful; by engaging in this practice, sages and brahmins "stand on dry ground"—that is, in a place of security and safety. Those who succeed in doing this training are characterized as knowing the Dharma. They are unshakable and even-minded, free of cruelty, greed, and agitation.

The second part of the poem, which contains the training verses, refers back to some of the concepts the Buddha mentions in the first five verses. Where the Buddha mentions how he was dismayed, shaken, and discontented, the training verses describe the goal as becoming free from agitation, unshaken, and peaceful. In contrast to the early verses where the Buddha says he could not find a place of his own, the training verses describe the sage as standing on dry ground. Rather than wanting a place of their own, the verses also state that sages do not take anything as "mine" and don't feel grief over the thought "I have nothing." Juxtaposed with the agitation that comes from seeing everything change, those who complete the training see safety everywhere. These pairings of opposites in the earlier and later verses suggest a deliberate rhetorical device. If this is so, then we can surmise that the arrow stuck in the heart is greed, selfish possessiveness, and having the sense of "mine." Having pulled these out, sages are "peaceful, unselfish."[1]

ATTADAṆḌA SUTTA
The Discourse on Being Violent

Violence gives birth to fear;
[Just] look at people and [their] quarrels.
I will speak of my dismay[2]
And the way that I was shaken.[3]

[935]

Seeing people thrashing about
  Like fish in little water,
  And seeing them feuding with each other,
  I became afraid.

[936]

The world is completely without a core.
  Everywhere things are changing.[4]
  Wanting a place of my own,
  I saw nothing not already taken.

[937]

I felt discontent at seeing
  Only conflict to the very end.
  Then I saw an arrow here,
  Hard to see, embedded in the heart.

[938]

Pierced by this arrow,
  [People] dash about in all directions.
  When the arrow's pulled out
  They don't run, and they don't sink.

[939]

(Here the trainings are recited):[5]
Don't pursue
  What the world's knotted up in.
  Having fully pierced sensuality,
  Train in your own full release.[6]

[940]

Truthful, not impudent or deceitful,
Anger-free and never speaking divisively,
A sage would overcome
Avarice and the evil of greed.

[941]

One should conquer drowsiness, laziness, and sluggishness,
And not live negligently.
A person intent on full release
Should not be conceited.

[942]

One should not be pulled into false speech
Or become enamored with physical forms.
One should fully understand conceit
And refrain from a violent life.[7]

[943]

One shouldn't delight in the old
Or prefer the new.
One shouldn't grieve what's lost,
Or cling to what's attractive.[8]

[944]

Greed I call "the great flood"
And desire, a "swift [current]."
Objects of awareness are "moving [waves],"
And lust is a "quagmire difficult to cross."

[945]

Not deviating from truth
Sages, brahmins, stand on dry ground.
Giving up everything,
They are said to be at peace.

[946]

Knowing, they are "Ones-Who-Know."
Knowing the Dharma, they are not dependent.
Wandering properly through the world,
They do not envy anyone here.

[947]

They who here have overcome lust,
—a clinging hard to overcome in this world—
Don't grieve or worry.
They have cut the stream, they are unbound.

[948]

What was before—let it wither away!
What will be later—do nothing with it!
Not grasping what's in between
You'll live at peace.

[949]

By not taking as *mine*
Anything that is "name and appearance,"
And not grieving what doesn't exist,[9]
One is not diminished in this world.

[950]

Who doesn't say "this is mine"
  Or that anything [belongs] to others[10]
  Doesn't experience selfishness
  And doesn't grieve [thinking] "I have nothing."

[951]

When asked, I say
  The benefit of being unshakable
  Is being even-minded everywhere
  And being without cruelty, greed, and agitation.

[952]

For one who knows, who has no agitation,
  There is no [karmic] accumulation.[11]
  Abstaining from [karmic] activity,
  One sees safety everywhere.

[953]

Sages do not say they are
  Inferior, superior, or equal [to others].
  Peaceful, unselfish,
  They neither embrace nor reject.

[954]

CHAPTER 16

The Discourse to Sāriputta

Monastic Training

This final poem in the *Book of Eights*—"The Discourse to Sāriputta"—is markedly different in tone and content from the preceding poems in the anthology. In the introduction, I discussed the book's four major themes—clinging to views, sensual desire, the qualities of the sage, and the training of monastics. This poem is the only discourse in the collection that focuses exclusively on monastic training, with no mention of the other three themes.

Furthermore, this poem contains concepts not found in the other fifteen poems. For example, the goal of monastic training is here described as "awakening" (*saṃbodhi*) and "obliterating the darkness," concepts that are more abstract than the personal, psychological qualities used to describe the sage in the preceding discourses. This poem is also the only one that contains the word *Buddha* in the verses themselves. It also has the sole occurrence of the title "Perfect Dharma" (*sammā dhammā*).

The poem introduces the Buddha's chief disciple, Sāriputta, who speaks the first eight verses of the discourse. Some scholars believe Sāriputta's introductory verses are a later addition to the poem, an idea supported by the fact that these verses are composed in a different meter than the section attributed to the Buddha.[1] Consistent with this hypothesis, these verses introduce concepts not found elsewhere in the *Book of Eights.* In the course of praising the Buddha, Sāriputta mentions gods; reference is also made to the Buddha coming from *Tuṣita* heaven, meaning that in the lifetime before becoming the Buddha, he was a deity living in a particular heavenly realm. This mention of the unseen world of gods and heavens is out of keeping with the rest of the anthology, where there's a complete absence of these sorts of references, emphasizing instead present-moment behavior and personal qualities. It stands in contrast to the teachings the Buddha gives in the remaining verses of this particular poem as well. Also noteworthy is Sāriputta's use of the the title "Buddha," a word otherwise absent throughout the *Book of Eights.*

When he asks the Buddha to provide instruction in monastic training, Sāriputta asks what precepts (*sīla*) and religious practices (*vata*) monastics should undertake. This, too, is a departure from the rest of the discourses. Elsewhere in the verses, the Buddha deemphasizes the role of precepts and religious practices. For example, he describes the sage (and true brahmin) as one who is independent of precepts and religious practices (verses 799, 803, and 839). Yet here, Sāriputta is equating Buddhist practices with these very activities.

If the earlier discourses in the *Book of Eights* actually advocate activities we can call "religious practice," they do so primarily in terms of what sages don't do and what they should *abandon* doing. This emphasis changes with "The Discourse to Sāriputta," where the Buddha presents a series of actions that monastics should perform and a number of attitudes they should adopt. Monastics should be firm in their exertion, revere wisdom, enjoy what's admirable, be satisfied, engage in meditative absorption, be ever wakeful and collected, be happy when reprimanded, freely offer skillful words, examine the right Dharma, and become unified. In addition, monastics should "touch with loving-kindness those who tremble and those who are firm."

Although this discourse differs in many ways from the others, it bears the most similarity to "The Discourse on Being Quick" (Chapter 14). Both poems explicitly emphasize monastic training. They are also the only discourses in the collection that contain praise for the Buddha; perhaps revering the Buddha is an important attitude for monastics who have not yet attained the goal of practice, as they still rely on the Buddha and his teachings to guide their training. That the teachings here are for those who are still training is seen in such instructions as "they should remove these despairing thoughts" and "they should vanquish discontent."

If all the discourses in the *Book of Eights* are assembled to present a coordinated message, then it seems that the overall arc of the teachings goes from describing the ideal sage in the early chapters to providing instruction for becoming a sage in the later chapters. The goal, presented in very human terms, is mentioned first. The means to the goal follows.

Sāriputta Sutta
The Discourse for Sāriputta

(Sāriputta said,)
"Never before have I seen or heard a teacher
With such lovely speech,
Who has come from Tuṣita
For the many [people here].

[955]

"The One-with-Eyes appears
To the world with its gods;
Having dispelled the darkness,
He has attained delight by himself alone.

[956]

"To that Buddha who is independent, not deceitful,
Who is Thus,[2]
Who has come with his followers,
I ask a question for those in bondage here.

[957]

"For a disaffected[3] monastic
Who frequents empty sitting places,
The foot of trees, cemeteries,
And mountain caves,

[958]

"How many terrors are there,
At which a monastic shouldn't tremble,
Sleeping in high and low [places],
Living in quiet [places]?

[959]

"How many dangers of the world
Should be mastered by the monastic,
Living in remote dwellings,
Going where never gone before?[4]

[960]

"For resolute monastics,
How should they speak?
What should be the field [of their activity]?
What should be their precepts and religious practices?

[961]

"What training should they take on,
Those who are solitary,[5] wise, and mindful,
To purify their own impurities
As a silversmith would those of silver?"[6]

[962]

("Sāriputta," said the Blessed One,)
"I will tell you, you who [already] knows,
What is comfort for someone disaffected
Who frequents secluded places,
Who desires Awakening in accord with the Dharma.

[963]

"Wise monastics, mindful and living restrained[7]
Shouldn't fear the five fears:
Horseflies, mosquitoes, snakes,
Human contact,[8] and four-footed beings.

[964]

"They shouldn't fear followers of other teachings
Even when seeing much that is frightful in them.
Seeking what's skillful,
They should overcome still other dangers.

[965]

"They should endure cold and extreme heat
And contact with sickness, hunger, and thirst.
Touched by these in many ways
They, homeless ones, should make effort
And be firm in their exertion.[9]

[966]

"They shouldn't steal or lie.
They should touch with loving-kindness
Those who tremble and those who are firm.
Whatever disturbance they know in their minds
They should dispel [thinking,]
'[It belongs to] the dark side.'

[967]

"They shouldn't be influenced by anger and conceit;
They should live[10] having uprooted these.
Masters,[11] they would overcome
What's cherished and what's not.

[968]

"Revering wisdom, delighting in what's admirable,[12]
They should eliminate those dangers.
In remote settings they should vanquish discontent.
They should conquer the four [reasons for] despair:

[969]

'What will I eat?'
'Where will I eat?'
'I have slept so badly!'
'Where will I sleep tonight?'

"Those who wander homeless,
Who are in training,
Should remove these despairing thoughts.

[970]

"Receiving food and clothing at the [right] time,
They know what's enough for satisfaction.
Guarded in these things and restrained in villages,
Even when offended, they say nothing harsh.

[971]

"Eyes downcast, not agitated,[13] practicing meditation,[14]
They should be ever wakeful.
Composed and equanimous,
They should cut off doubt and worry.

[972]

"Mindful, they would be happy when reprimanded.
They would destroy their surliness[15] toward others in the holy life.
They would speak skillfully but not excessively.
And not think about things people gossip about.

[973]

"Furthermore, mindfully they should train
To remove the five stains of the world:
They should conquer passion[16]
For forms, sounds, tastes, smells and touch.

[974]

"Monastics, mindful with well-liberated minds,
Would subdue desire for these things.
Examining the Perfect[17] Dharma at the right time,
Becoming concentrated,[18] they should obliterate the darkness."

[975]

Afterword

While the earliest evidence indicates that the *Book of Eights* was originally an independent work, for at least fifteen hundred years it has been housed as one of the five sections (*vaggas*) of an anthology of scriptures called the *Sutta Nipāta* or *Discourse Section.*[1] The *Sutta Nipāta,* in turn, is one of sixteen texts placed within a larger anthology called the *Minor Collection* (*Khuddaka Nikāya*), which is itself one of five collections of texts that make up the *Sutta Piṭaka,* or the *Basket of Discourses.* By one count, the entire *Basket of Discourses* contains approximately eighteen thousand individual texts purporting to be the direct teachings of either the Buddha or his disciples. The *Basket of Discourses* is one of three "Baskets" that contain the sacred canon of Theravada Buddhism, the primary form of Buddhism in the South and Southeast Asian countries of Sri Lanka, Myanmar, Thailand, Laos, and Cambodia.

Because the modern scholarly study of this vast body of literature is still relatively young, we do not yet have a clear understanding of when many of these texts were composed. It is likely that some—possibly many—of the teachings and texts attributed to the Buddha were composed well after he died. One of the "holy grails" in the study of ancient Buddhism is to discover which of the ancient discourses might date from the time of the Buddha and so might represent his actual teachings, before they evolved in the centuries after his death. While a variety of theories have been proposed for distinguishing which discourses are chronologically early, intermediate, or late, the rationale for these theories are not widely accepted.

Even so, the *Book of Eights* is broadly (but not universally) accepted as a prime candidate for inclusion among the earliest surviving Buddhist literature. Two other texts, also found in the *Sutta Nipāta,* are often considered to have the same antiquity as the *Book of Eights*: the poem "The Rhinoceros Horn" (*Khaggavisāṇa Sutta*), and most of the anthology called the *Book of the Way to the Other Shore* (*Pārāyanavagga*).[2] One reason these are believed to be early is that they make no reference to settled monastic communities and so may represent a time early in the Buddha's teaching career when he and his monastics were peripatetic wanderers. However, it seems that many Buddhist monastics were intermittent wanderers during and after the Buddha's lifetime, with some practitioners more dedicated to this lifestyle than others. Rather than suggesting an early date of composition, the lack of reference to settled monastic communities could mean the text was composed during one of the times that the Buddha or others were wandering.

Linguistic evidence provides additional, compelling reasons to postulate that these poems are among the earliest Buddhist literature. The meter, grammar, and vocabulary found in many of the poems are old. Some words, declensions, and conjugations in the *Book of Eights* do not appear anywhere else in the Buddhist scriptures. However, because poets may use well-established and long-standing poetic elements for aesthetic effect or maintaining meter, the antiquity of some of these linguistic elements is not sufficient evidence for determining the age of the poems. Additionally, because linguistic developments may have evolved at different times in different areas, the *Book of Eights* may have been composed in a different location than most of the other early Buddhist scriptures, and this could explain the use of unique words or conjugations.

The *Book of Eights,* "The Rhinoceros Horn," and the sixteen discourses in the *Book of the Way to the Other Shore* have a canonical commentary called the *Analytical Explanation* (*Niddesa*). The fact that this commentary was included in the *Khuddaka Nikāya* section of the canon is an indicator that the poems were composed well before the canon was closed. However, we have no solid evidence suggesting when the canon was actually closed. A brief mention in the fifth century C.E. states that the canon was first written down in the first century B.C.E. Some have inferred from this that the canon was completed and closed by the first century B.C.E. But we do not, in fact, have solid evidence that the canon was fixed in its present form until about the fifth century when extant commentaries of the canon were written. The *Analytical Explanation* was surely written prior to the fifth century C.E. Scholars have suggested that this commentary was composed sometime between the third century B.C.E. and the first century C.E.[3] This wide range does not give us reliable evidence to support the idea that the *Book of Eights* belongs to the very earliest historical strata of Buddhist texts, a strata sometimes called "primitive Buddhism" or "precanonical Buddhism."

Another basis for assuming the *Book of Eights* was composed earlier than some of the other discourses in the *Basket of Discourses* is that two *suttas* mention these poetic anthologies by name.[4] As we don't know the dates that the two *suttas* were composed, all we can reliably assert is that the anthology is older than the discourses that mention them.

An ancient stone inscription that dates from the third century B.C.E. seems to mention by name one of the poems from the *Book of Eights.* This is found in an edict composed by King Asoka, who ruled much of India from about 269 B.C.E. to 232 B.C.E.[5] The inscription mentions a text titled *Upatisa-pasine*—that is, "Upatisa's Question." Because the similar name, Upatissa, is the personal name of Sāriputta ("the son of Sāri"), this text is tentatively identified as the *Sāriputta Sutta,* the last discourse in the *Book of Eights,* a text in which Sāriputta poses a question to the Buddha. If these two titles refer to the same text, then the *Sāriputta Sutta* would have been composed sometime before 232 B.C.E. The value of this cautious suggestion is increased with the observation that King Asoka's inscription provides the earliest epigraphical evidence for the existence of any Buddhist text.

Still another argument that the *Book of Eights* was composed earlier than most of the other early scriptures relies on the absence of the numerical organization of Buddhist teachings that is common in much of the Buddhist canonical literature. To emphasize a point made in the introduction, I would like to again mention that the *Book of Eights* contains no mention of such core Buddhist doctrines as the Three Characteristics, the Four Noble Truths, the Four Levels of Concentration, the Five Faculties, the Six Sense Bases, the Seven Factors of Awakening, the Eightfold Path, or the Twelvefold Conditions of Dependent Origination. Also, the *Book of Eights* does not refer to psychic powers or depict the Buddha in any supernatural way, a trend that grew over the centuries after the Buddha died. The argument is that these teachings are not mentioned because they were not yet formulated. This, however, ignores the fact that different genres of texts may emphasize very different ideas. Poetry, for example, is not a common place for referring to numerical lists.

Perhaps it is the sum total of all these reasons that provides the best case for the *Book of Eights*' antiquity. But even if we accept that this may be a record of the Buddha's earliest teachings, we should remember that the tradition holds that the Buddha taught for some forty-five years. This is long enough for him to have developed, elaborated, and systematized his teachings. The fact that some teachings might have been early does not mean that they should be automatically prioritized over later teachings as better representing the Buddha's core message.

While we can't be sure where to place the *Book of Eights* in the timeline of early Buddhist India, we do have evidence that its teachings were valued by the early Indian Buddhists. As pointed out in the introduction, the *Book of Eights* belongs to a small group of poems that the early Buddhists selected for memorization, recitation, and teaching. These poems seem to represent teachings that some early practitioners, perhaps even the Buddha himself, choose to emphasize.

I propose that among the many discourses found in the anthologies of canonical scriptures, the ones that best represent teachings important to early Buddhists are those that those Buddhists themselves chose to emphasize. We can determine which ones these are by looking at which texts were referred to or commented on within other canonical texts. As noted earlier, the *Book of Eights* is referred to a number of times in these works. The existence of the early *Niddesa* commentary further suggests the *Book of Eights* was important during the early centuries of Buddhism in India.

The importance or influence of the *Book of Eights* is not restricted to the Theravada tradition (the Buddhist tradition that has preserved the Pali canon) or even early Buddhism. References to the *Book of Eights* are made in literature belonging to other Buddhist schools or lineages in ancient India. In addition to the Theravada school, the literature of the Sarvāstivāda, Mūla-Sarvāstivāda, and the Dharmaguptaka schools all mention the text by name.[6] Indian Mahayana literature, such as Asanga's *Bodhisattvabhumi,* also refers to the *Book of Eights,* indicating that it had an enduring role among Indian Buddhists well into the Common Era. All these references suggest that the *Book of Eights* was a valued text for many centuries. Because these texts mention the *Book of Eights* without referring to the *Sutta Nipāta,* it is likely that it was considered an independent work.

As a sacred scripture for a number of Buddhist schools, the *Book of Eights* was preserved in a variety of Indic languages. The Pali-language version of the Theravada canon is just one version of several that once existed. Unfortunately, only one other complete version survives. This is a Chinese translation done in the third century C.E. from an unknown Indic language.[7] Sections of the *Book of Eights* exist in Sanskrit—some as quotations in Buddhist texts such as Vasbandhu's *Abhidharma-kośa* and Asanga's *Bodhisattva-bhumi.* Manuscript fragments in the Indic language of Gandharan have been retrieved from the Gandharan region of Pakistan.

The existence of the *Book of Eights* in different languages raises questions about the original title of the work. In Sanskrit texts, it is usually called the *Book of Meaning* (*Arthavargīya* or *Arthavargīyāni*), but sometimes it is the *Book of Eights* (*Aṣṭavarga*). While it is customary to understand *aṭṭha* in the Pali *Aṭṭhakavagga* to mean "eight," the word also means "meaning," "goal," and "benefit." Consequently we can't be certain what the title might have originally been. One theory is that the title *Book of Eights* is derived from the four poems that have eight verses each. That the title of each of these poems contains the word *eightfold* reinforces this idea. This possibility has led to the subsequent theory that the original core of the anthology was these four poems (chapters 2 through 5).

Regardless of the original title, it is possible that some of the sixteen poems of the *Book of Eights* may have existed as independent works before being added to the anthology. Others may be closely related, perhaps having been composed by the same person(s). Most closely associated with each other are the four poems that have eight verses each, all composed with the same poetic meter. That three of these texts—chapters 3, 4, and 5—have similar teachings also suggests a close association.

While the Theravada tradition assumes that all the Buddhist teachings in the *Book of Eights* are spoken by the Buddha, most of the poems do not specifically mention the Buddha. In a few of the poems, early editors added interlinear notes indicating who they believed spoke certain verses. Some of these notes indicate that the Buddha is the speaker. We know that these editorial additions are relatively early because they are mentioned in the *Niddesa*.[8] In my translation, these interlinear notes are placed in parentheses. By contrast, notes identifying the speaker that are in square brackets are my interpretations, which I added to aid in clarity. Without these additions by the early editors or by me, only three of the sixteen poems specifically indicate that they contain verses attributed to the Buddha (chapters 10, 14, and 16). Beyond the *Book of Eights,* a layperson speaking to Mahā Kaccāna in the *Hāliddakāni Sutta,* attributes the *Māgaṇḍiya Sutta* (chapter 9) to the Buddha.[9]

In the Pali scriptures, Mahā Kaccāna is uniquely

associated with the *Book of Eights,* as it is only he who provides a commentary or interpretation for a verse from the anthology (in the aforementioned *Hāliddakāni Sutta*). It is his disciple Soṇa who recites the entire *Book of Eights* when the Buddha asks him to present teachings.[10] The *Soṇa Sutta's* story of Soṇa's discipleship under Mahā Kaccāna suggests that Soṇa most likely learned the *Book of Eights* from Mahā Kaccāna, because there were almost no other monks in Avanti, the region where Soṇa and Mahā Kaccāna lived.

Some of the teachings in *suttas* associated with Mahā Kaccāna have enough similarities with teachings found in the *Book of Eights* to suggest a connection between them. For example, one *sutta* passage opens with Mahā Kaccāna being asked a question similar to the opening of the *Kalahavivāda Sutta* of the *Book of Eights.* His response echoes the discussions in the *Book of Eights* about renunciants arguing with each other about their doctrine. Mahā Kaccāna explains that aristocrats, brahmins, and householders quarrel because of lust for sensual pleasure, but renunciants do so because of lust for views.[11]

Mahā Kaccāna is also associated with the Honeyball Sutta, a discourse in the *Majjhima Nikāya* in which the Buddha gives surprisingly similar teachings using a similar vocabulary to that in the *Book of Eights* but distinct from much of the rest of the *suttas.* After the Buddha's brief teaching in this text, Mahā Kaccāna provides a lengthy explanation.[12] In the same vein, Mahā Kaccāna also provides an exposition on "An Auspicious Day," a poem with teachings related to what is found in the *Book of*

Eights.[13] The occasion for Mahā Kaccāna's explanation was a request from a Samiddhi, a monk who elsewhere in the canon is partly responsible for the Buddha reciting a verse found in the *Book of Eights.*[14]

Overall, the teachings by Mahā Kaccāna found in the Pali *suttas* are all similar to the teachings in the *Book of Eights* in lacking the standard language and frameworks usually employed to characterize the early Buddhist teachings. Neither group of texts refers to the Four Noble Truths, the Eightfold Path, the Four Foundations of Mindfulness, the Seven Factors of Awakening, or the Twelvefold Factors of Dependent Origination. Both teach liberation without any reference to future lives or ending rebirth. That these teachings are absent in the *Book of Eights* is therefore not something unique to this anthology of poems.

The direct and indirect associations of Mahā Kaccāna with the *Book of Eights* suggest that the anthology may well represent the teaching emphasis of one person or group. Rather than being chronologically earlier relative to some other early Buddhist teachings, the *Book of Eights* may have its origin with a particular Buddhist group in a particular location. The close association of Mahā Kaccāna with the country of Avanti in Western India raises the question of whether the anthology may have been composed or collected in a region remote from the center of early Buddhism in Northeastern India.

This is, of course, speculation. We know very little about the genesis of the early Buddhist teachings, including the origin of the *Book of Eights.* Perhaps this uncertainty is appropriate. The *Book of Eights* contains inspiring teachings pointing to the possibility of peace when we release all of our clinging, including clinging to views about religious teachings. It is a peace that is not dependent on knowing whether or not these teachings represent the earliest teachings of the Buddha. For practitioners, it is a peace that authenticates itself.

APPENDIX

Knowing and Seeing in the *Book of Eights*

Knowing and seeing are primary activities associated with the ideal sage in the *Book of Eights.* This appendix gathers many of the lines of verse that emphasize these activities. Glancing through these quotes will highlight how frequently knowing and seeing are mentioned and how important these activities were for the composers of these poems.

For a full study of the role of knowing and seeing, one should also study the many statements discouraging attachment to what is seen or known.

Positive Statements about Knowing

Don't do what you **know**
  is out of harmony in the world

Fully **understanding** concepts and having crossed the
flood
Sages don't cling to possessions.

[779]

Great sages, having **known** by means of knowledge,
Having understood the Dharma,
Don't experience highs and lows.

[792]

With death, people lose
What they conceive as "mine."
Knowing this, a sage should not
Be selfishly devoted to what is "mine."

[806]

Knowing these dangers here
A sage—both earlier and later—
Should become firm in the single life
And not indulge in sex.

[821]

What is the meaning of this "inner peace"?
How is it made **known** by the wise?

[838]

Those who **know** don't become proud
In regard to views or what is thought out.

[846]

Having **known** the Dharma, they are independent.

[856]

Whoever is uncertain should train in the way of
knowledge,
For it is from having **known** that the Renunciant
spoke of mental states.

[868]

Knowing, "[both] these [claims] are conditional,"
A sage investigates conditionality.
Knowing, the liberated one doesn't get into
disputes.

[877]

One who **knows** doesn't get involved
In any particular opinion

[897]

Knowing the many commonplace opinions
They are equanimous, thinking, "That is what
others hold on to."

[911]

Knowing this Dharma, inquiring monastics,
Always mindful, would train [in it].
Knowing release is peace,
They wouldn't neglect Gotama's message.

[933]

Knowing, they are "Ones-Who-Know."
Knowing the Dharma, they are not dependent.

[947]

For one who **knows,** who has no agitation,
There is no [karmic] accumulation.

[953]

Whatever disturbance they **know** in their minds,
They should dispel [thinking,]
"[It belongs to] the dark side."

[967]

Receiving food and cloth at the [right] time,
They **know** what's enough for satisfaction.

[971]

Positive Statements about Seeing

Therefore, having abandoned grasping,
Sages live **seeing** safety.

[809]

Renunciants are elated and deflated
By the disputes that arise among them.
Seeing this, you should abstain from disputes—
They provide no benefit other than being praised.

[828]

Seeing craving, aversion, and lust
I have no desire for sex.

[835]

Seeing—but not grasping—these views,
I knew and saw inner peace.

[837]

Not clinging to the future,
Nor grieving the past,
They **see** seclusion in the midst of sense contacts
And are not guided by views.

[851]

Having observed this, one shouldn't dispute,
Seeing safety is the place without disputes.

[896]

I ask you, O Kinsman of the Sun, Great **Seer,**
About seclusion and the state of peace.

[915]

The one with open eyes, the **Eyewitness** to the Dharma,
Proclaims the removal of danger.

[921]

He is the Unconquered Conqueror,
  Eyewitness to the Dharma
  Who **saw** without relying on hearsay.

[934]

Then I **saw** an arrow here,
  Hard to **see**, embedded in the heart.

[938]

Abstaining from [karmic] activity,
  One **sees** safety everywhere.

[953]

Notes

Introduction

1. The most common word for "peace," *santi,* occurs sixteen times. "Equanimity," or *upekkha,* occurs four times.
2. In my translation, I use "clinging" to translate *saṅgaṃ, anuggahaaya, samugghaaya, paṭilīyati, limpati,* and *upādi.* "Craving" is used to translate *taṇha, ejā,* and *visattika.* "Entrenched" is used to translate *nivesana, niviṭṭha,* and *thāma.* "Quarreling" is used to translate *vivāda, viggaha, viggayha,* and *medhaga.*
3. Tilmann Vetter, "Mysticism in the Aṭṭhakavagga," in *The Ideas and Meditative Practices of Early Buddhism* (Leiden, The Netherlands: E. J. Brill, 1988), 101–6.
4. Eviatar Shulman, "Early Buddhist Imagination: The *Aṭṭhakavagga* as Buddhist Poetry," *Journal of the International Association of Buddhist Studies* 35, no. 1 (2012–2013): 363.
5. The *Hāliddakāni Sutta* 1 from the *Collected Discourses of the Buddha* (*Saṃyutta Nikāya*) 22.3.
6. The *Soṇa Sutta* is found in the *Udana* 5.6. Soṇa and his reciting of the *Book of Eights* also appears in the *Vinaya* (*Mahāvagga* V, 13.10).

7. "The Discourse on the Noble Quest" (*Ariyapariyesanā Sutta* from the *Middle Length Discourses* MN I, 168).
8. *Nandamātā Sutta* from the *Numerical Discourses of the Buddha* (*Aṅguttara Nikāya* 7.53).
9. The poem, titled *Bhaddekaratta* in Pali, is found in the discourses in the *Middle Length Discourses* numbered 131, 132, 133, and 134.
10. *Madhupiṇḍika Sutta* from the *Majjhima Nikāya* 18 (I 108). "Concepts" is a translation for *sañña*, which is also how I have translated this word in the *Book of Eights*.
11. *Madhupiṇḍika Sutta* from the *Majjhima Nikāya* 18 (I 109–110).
12. As discussed in the afterword to this book, most of the chapters in the *Book of Eights* do not explicitly state that it is the Buddha who provides the teachings. It's by tradition that all the teachings in the anthology are attributed to the Buddha.
13. Verses 788, 824, 891, 892, 898, 899, 901, 906, 908, and 910.
14. Verses 789, 790, 830, 834, and 876.
15. *Peace* and *peaceful* are mentioned in verses 789, 790, 807, 811, 828, 839, 843, 844, 845, 851, 853, 857, 861, 906, 912, 921, 925, 932, 938, 952, 955, and 960.
16. Brahmins are mentioned nine times in chapters 4, 5, 9, 10, 13, and 15. Renunciants are mentioned eight times in chapters 8, 10, 11, 12, and 14.
17. *Bṛhadāraṇyaka Upaniṣad* 3.5.1.
18. *Bṛhadāraṇyaka Upaniṣad* 3.5.1 and 4.4.22.
19. *Bṛhadāraṇyaka Upaniṣad 4.4.5–4.4.6.*
20. One example of this is a mention of the concept of "name and appearance" (*nāma-rūpa*). This is an ancient Indian expression used in a variety of ways in Buddhist

texts. While its Buddhist meaning has changed over time, it is commonly defined as referring to a person's physical and mental experience. Its use in the *Book of Eights* is closer to that of the pre-Buddhist literature than of later Buddhist texts.

21. Monastics (*bhikkhu*, occasionally translated as "mendicants") are mentioned eighteen times in chapters 3, 5, 6, 14, and 16.
22. *Tuvaṭṭaka-sutta-niddeso* (Nidd 2.343).
23. *Santipada* in verse 915, chapter 14.
24. For example, N. A. Jayawickrama, "Analysis of the Sutta Nipāta," *University of Ceylon Review* 6 (1948): 42–48.
25. *Kasibhāradvāja Sutta,* verse 82.
26. K. R. Norman, *The Group of Discourses* (Oxford: Pali Text Society, 2001), 122.
27. Hammalawa Saddhatissa, *The Sutta-Nipāta* (London: Curzon Press, 1985).
28. Andrew Olendzki, trans., "*Attadaṇḍa Sutta*: Arming Oneself," 2005, www.accesstoinsight.org/tipitaka/kn/snp/snp.4.15.olen.html.

Chapter 1: The Discourse on Desire

1. Verses 771, 779, 823, 857, and 945.
2. Two other unrelated discourses in the Pali discourses are called *Kāma Sutta* (*Saṃyutta Nikāya* i.44 and *Aṅguttara Nikāya* IV.458).
3. *Bṛhadāraṇyaka Upaniṣad* 4.4.7.
4. "Suffering pours in" is the translation of *Tato naṃ dukkhamanveti,* the third line in the first verse of the Dhammapada.

Chapter 2: The Eightfold Discourse on the Hiding Place

1. "Hiding place" is a translation for *guhā,* a word that can also mean "cave." It is likely that this word is used here to contrast the Buddha's teachings from some of the teachings found in the Upanishads, where *guhā* refers to the inner hidden sanctum where ultimate reality is found. Whereas verse 772 emphasizes the letting go of desires, the *Taittiriya Upaniṣad* (2.1) states that if one realizes the truth found in this inner sanctum, one will attain all desires: "A person knowing brahman, the truth, knowledge and the infinite as being in the hiding place within and in the highest heavens attains all desires together with brahman, the wise." See also *Kaṭha Upaniṣad* 1.14, 2.1, and 3.1.
2. "Disharmony" is the translation of *visama,* a word literally meaning "not even," that is sometimes translated as "wrong."
3. "Existence" is a translation for *bhava,* translated as "becoming" in the next line.
4. *Mamāyite;* this can also mean what one cherishes.
5. Continuing the ideas of the previous verses, "both sides" probably refers to states of becoming and nonbecoming.
6. *Phassa,* translated here as "sense experience," is more commonly translated as "contact" with the meaning of "sense contact"—that is, the direct stimulation of a sense organ through contact between the organ and a sense object.
7. "Concepts" is the translation of *sañña,* of which the common English translation is "perception." See the introduction to this book for a discussion of this term.

Chapter 3: The Eightfold Discourse on the Corrupt

1. The word *loka* occurs more than forty times in the *Book of Eights,* seventeen times with the expression "in the world."
2. *Khila,* translated here as "despondent," also means "barren."
3. *Abhinibbuta*: "fully stilled."
4. *Dhammā.*
5. *Dhammā.*
6. *Dhono*: "Those who are cleansed."

Chapter 4: The Eightfold Discourse on the Pure

1. The opening verse is the claim to which the rest of the poem responds. Because much of the response is critical of brahmins, I am suggesting the opening verse was spoken by a brahmin.
2. "Pure" is the translation of *suddha.* "Sees" is a translation for *diṭṭha.*
3. "Knowledge" is a translation of *ñāṇa.*
4. "Someone with attachments" is the translation of *sopadhīko,* a compound word derived from *sa* (with) and *upadhi. Upadhi* is an important word in the *suttas.* It can mean both "attachment" and "basis" or "foundation." In the latter sense, in later texts, it came to mean the attachments that are the basis for rebirth.
5. Or perhaps, "Then someone with attachments is purified by some thing or another." "Other" is the translation of *aññato.* It is not clear what is being referred to here. It is possible that the word should be taken to mean "a thing." In this case the line

would read, "Then for someone with attachments, purity would be caused by a thing." As the next verse suggests, purity doesn't come from a thing, it comes from the absence of things—for example, concern with merit and evil, involvement with self, and creating things.

6. "Virtue" is the translation of *sīla*; "[religious] observances" is the translation of *vata,* a term that can also mean "vows." I translate these words differently depending on the context.
7. "What is grasped" is the translation of *atta.* While this is a homonym with the Pali word for "self," the *Aṭṭhakavagga* does not emphasize teachings having to do with self and not-self. Because in contrast, it does emphasize clinging and freedom from clinging, I have chosen to translate *atta* as the past participle of *ādiyati*, meaning "takes," "seizes," or "grasps."
8. *Sañña.*
9. "Experiences" is the translation of *gacchati,* which most literally means "he/she goes."
10. "Knowledge" is the translation of *veda,* a word that also refers to the ancient, sacred texts that brahmins relied on for religious knowledge. As this verse is redefining what it means to be a brahmin (see verse 790), it is likely that the word *veda* is also being redefined in a new way to refer to personal insight.
11. "Assumptions" is the translation of *vikappayeyya,* which I take as an emphatic (with the prefix *vi*) form of *kappati,* here meaning "frames, imagines, contrives, or theorizes about."
12. "Whose conduct is open" is the translation of *vivaṭaṃ carantaṃ,* which may instead refer to "those who live

in the open"—that is, those renunciants who live the wandering life.

13. "Abandoned" is the translation of *visajja* by reading it as *vissajja.*
14. "Boundaries" is the translation of *sima,* which usually means "boundary" or a "bounded area." The traditional commentaries explain that it refers to the Ten Fetters (*samyojana*). It is likely that it refers to the strict boundaries within which brahmins lived in order to maintain purity. This included ritual boundaries and social boundaries that kept people of different castes and different degrees of presumed purity apart.
15. "Superior" is the translation of *parama*; the discourse opens and closes with this concept.

Chapter 5: The Eightfold Discourse on the Ultimate

1. "Inferior" is the translation of *hīna,* a powerful word that also means "despicable" or "base."
2. "Self" is the translation of *attanī* (*atta* in the locative case with a long *i* for the sake of the meter). If *atta* is being used without reference to Upanishadic ideas of the Self, the verse could be translated as "Seeing benefit in reference to oneself in things seen, heard, thought, . . ."
3. "Those who are skilled" is the translation of *kusalā.*
4. "Monastic" is the translation of *bhikkhu.*
5. In Pali, *atta* can mean either "what is taken up" or "self." I have chosen the former because it fits the context better.
6. "Concept" is the translation of *sañña.*
7. "Doctrine" is the translation of *dhammā.*
8. "Rely on belief" is the translation of *pacceti.* This word

literally means "to come on to" or "to come back to." It has the extended meaning of "to rely on" or "to believe in." The commentary to the *Aṭṭhakavagga* gives "to experience again" and "to slide back to" as synonyms. It explains that the brahmin won't fall back into defilement (*Mahāniddesa* I.5).

9. *Tādī.* For pre-Buddhist usage, see *Rig-Veda* V, 44.6.

Chapter 6: The Discourse on Old Age

1. "Mendicant" is a translation of *bhikkhu.* Because it is not obvious that this reference refers to Buddhist monastics, I use "mendicant" as a more inclusive word that can refer to any renunciant, Buddhist or otherwise.
2. "Unattached" is a translation of *patilīna,* a word derived from *līyati,* meaning "to stick" or "to cling"; *pati* is a prefix that here means "in opposition" or "against."
3. "Harmony" is a translation of *sāmaggiya.*
4. *Bhavane* ("dwelling") can mean either "becoming" or "a dwelling place." In the seven other occurrences of *bhavane* in the *suttas,* it clearly means "a dwelling place" or "a realm where someone resides." To be consistent with these other usages, I have translated the noun as "dwelling."
5. "Independent" is a translation of *anissito*: *a* ("not") + *nissito* ("dependent on, attached to, supported by").
6. "Cherished" is a translation of *piya,* which can also mean "what is dear, beloved, liked, or agreeable."
7. "Those who are cleansed" is the translation of *dhono.* As a title for a sage, the word is rarely used in the *suttas,* occurring only here and in verse 786 of the *Book of Eights.*

Chapter 7: The Discourse to Tissa Metteyya

1. This attribution and the next are unlikely to have been part of the original poem. They do not fit with the poem's meter. They are mentioned in the *Niddesa,* the early commentary on the *Book of Eights.* One idea is that they are notes relevant for recitation of the poem.
2. "Sex" is a translation of *methuna,* literally "sexual intercourse."
3. "Base" is a translation of *hīna.* Earlier I translated this word as "inferior." This passage is suggestive of the stronger meaning of the word.
4. "Free" is a translation of *ritta,* which also has connotations of being devoid or empty of something.

Chapter 9: The Discourse to Māgaṇḍiya

1. These teachings on not relying on views, learning, knowledge, virtue and [religious] observances are quite similar to teachings found in "Nanda's Questions," chapter 7 of the *Book of the Way to the Other Shore.*
2. "Craving, aversion, and lust" are translations of the words *taṇha, arati,* and *rāgai* respectively.
3. "[That] I don't want to touch even with my foot" is a translation of the phrase *pādāpi naṃ samphusituṃ na icche.* Because no specific gender is specified, I have avoided using the pronoun "her," which most translators supply in English translations of this phrase.
4. It seems *anuggahāya* could have two meanings: "not grasping" and "compassionate." Is this a play on words?
5. "Wise" is a translation of *dhiro,* a word that also has connotations of being firm.
6. Views, learning (*sutiya*), knowledge, virtue, and

observances are all in the instrumental case, i.e., the grammatical form a noun takes to indicate that the noun is instrument or means for an action. In addition to this instrumental use, this case also can mean "in terms of." Interpretations of this passage depend on which of these two meanings this case is applied to this passage. Elsewhere I have translated *sīlabbata* as "virtue and religious practices." In this context I believe Māgaṇḍiya is asking about brahmanical practices.

7. My translation of Māgaṇḍiya's words is based on the idea that he misunderstood the Buddha by understanding the instrumental case in its most common usage as the expression "by means of." From his use of the instrumental, it makes sense that Māgaṇḍiya thinks this is a foolish teaching.
8. "Notion" is a translation of *sañña*. Elsewhere, I have translated it as "concept."
9. The verse is also found in *Saṃyutta Nikāya* 1.20 (verse 48).
10. This verse is quoted as from the *Book of Eights* in the *Hāliddakāni Sutta* (*Saṃyutta Nikāya*, 22.3).
11. "Mighty one" is a translation of *nāga*.
12. "Those who know" is a translation of *vedagū,* a title for those who have reached (*gu*) knowledge (*veda*).
13. "Concepts" is a translation of *saññā*.

Chapter 10: The Discourse on Before Breaking Apart

1. "Death" (*bheda*) literally means "dissolution" and "breaking apart." As this is what happens at death, it sometimes means death or dying. *Bheda* is translated as death in verse 849.

2. "Behaving" is a translation of *sīla,* which usually means "virtue" or "virtuous conduct."
3. For the sake of clarity, in this verse I have translated *bheda* as "death," not literally as "breaking apart."
4. "Teach" is a translation of *mantabhāṇī,* literally "reciting mantra." *Mantra* can have various meanings, including sacred texts or speech, a Vedic verse or phrase, a charm or spell, or advice. The mention of "reciting" suggests the ancient Buddhist practice of memorizing and reciting Buddhist teachings—as in the *Book of Eights* itself. It is also possible that with its reference to mantras, this verse has an implied criticism of the Brahmanical practice of chanting Vedic mantras.
5. "Clinging" is a translation of *paṭilīyati* (*pati* = "back to, against, opposite"; *līyati* = "to stick, adhere, cling to").
6. This line is a translation of *na saddho na virajjati,* which could literally be translated as "A person without faith who doesn't free himself from passion." This is probably intended to be a surprising statement that implied the opposite—that is, "A person beyond faith, who is beyond needing to be free from passion."
7. *Attam,* and therefore *nir-attam,* has two possible meanings in Pali. It is not certain which is meant here. Perhaps both meanings are intended. *Attam* can mean both "self" and what is taken up or assumed. Since the teaching of not-self appears to be absent in the *Book of Eights,* I have translated it according to the second meaning.
8. "Talk" is a translation of *vāda,* which can also mean "dispute," "discussion," "teaching," or "viewpoint."
9. "Being free of comparisons, they do not compare" is an interpretive translation of *kappaṃ neti akappiyo.*

The Pali passage is difficult to understand. *Kappa* can mean what is proper, acceptable, or lawful. It can also mean "to theorize or imagine." In translating the word as "compare," I am reading it as continuing the description of the sages who do not categorize or imagine themselves as superior, equal, or inferior to others. This may refer to the ancient Indian practice of viewing people in hierarchical relationship to each other—that is, arranging people in their proper place. *Akappiyo* refers to someone who doesn't compare. Adding to the difficulty of translation, *kappa* also means "an eon," "a long period of time," or simply "time."

Chapter 11: The Discourse on Quarrels and Disputes

1. "Cherished" is a translation of *piya.*
2. "Future [state]" is a translation of *samparāya.*
3. "Desires" is a translation of *chanda.*
4. "Foundation" is a translation of *nidāna.*
5. "Mental qualities" is a translation of *dhammā.* Some translators render the word here as "states."
6. "Agreeable" and "disagreeable" are translations of *sātam* and *asātam,* respectively.
7. "Appearances" is a translation of *rūpā,* a word sometimes referring to material forms or to materiality in general.
8. "Way of knowledge" is a translation *ñāṇapatha.*
9. "Grasping" is a translation of *parigahā,* which can also mean "possessions" or "acquisitions."
10. "Name" and "appearance" are translations of *nāma* and *rūpa,* respectively. In Buddhist texts, *rūpa* is commonly translated as "form," often with the implication of physical objects, including the human body. Because of

the way the disappearance of *rūpa* is discussed in verse 874, it is more likely that *rūpa* in this poem is understood as being a product of the conceptualizing activity of the mind.

11. "Not conceiving concepts" is a translation of *na sañña saññi.*
12. "False concepts" is a translation of *visañña,* relying on the Pali Text Society Dictionary. In reference to passages in the Jātakas and commentaries, the dictionary also defines it as "unconscious." In this case, perhaps it can be translated as "the absence of conceiving."
13. "Conceptual differentiation" is a translation of *papañca saṅkhā.* Often translated as "proliferation," I do not believe that *papañca* here refers to the spread of abstract thinking. Rather it refers to the basic, perceptual act of distinguishing one object from another. A good example of this meaning is in the *Mahākoṭṭhita Sutta* (*Aṅguttara Nikāya* 4.173; ii 161). *Saṅkhā* refers to words, concepts, or definitions. The two terms together refer to the conceptual distinctions responsible for differentiating the field of perception. As such, they could also refer to the primordial differentiation of the undifferentiated universe.
14. "Of the spirit" is a translation of *yakkhassa. Yakkha* usually refers to a spirit being: for example, a tree spirit is called a *yakkha.* The term can also be used to refer to a person, presumably as a term of high respect. In this case, it probably refers to the Buddha. *Yakkha* can also refer to the "spirit" or "soul" of a person—that is, the person's *atta* (Sanskrit: *ātman*). In either case, it seems the question is whether the Buddha represents the highest degree of purity possible.

15. "No residue of grasping" is a translation of *an* ("not") + *upādi* + *sesa* ("remaining"). *Upādi* is difficult to translate, not least because it has many applied meanings. Most literally, it means "grasping." It also refers to the living, physical body a person has that was a product of past grasping and that continues while a person who is liberated from all grasping is still alive. The verse presents two views about purity. First, that the most purity a person can attain is what is possible while alive. The second is that the highest purity comes when one dies and all remnants of past grasping disappear.
16. "Conditional" is the translation of *upanissitā,* a term related to the Sanskrit word *upaniṣad.* In the *Bṛhadāraṇyaka Upaniṣad,* the word *upaniṣad* is used in two ways. Primarily it refers to the texts known as the Upanishads (as in *Bṛhadāraṇyaka Upaniṣad* 2.4.10). It can also mean "hidden connection"; see Patrick Olivelle, *The Early Upanishads* (London: Oxford University Press, 2014), 185.
17. "Associate" is a translation of *sameti,* a verb in the present tense with many meanings. It can mean to associate, to come together, to meet, to agree, and to know.

Chapter 12: The Shorter Discourse on the Dead End

1. I have translated *vyūha* (the *v* becomes a *b* in compound words) as "dead end" based on the *Pali-English Dictionary's* definition that it can mean a side street or cul-de-sac.
2. The rhetorical device of expressing what others believe

is used elsewhere in the *Book of Eights* (for example, verses 879–882).

3. "Concept" is a translation of *sañña.*
4. "Imperfect" is a translation of *akevali.*
5. "Doctrine" is a translation of *dhammā.*
6. "Truth" is a translation of *tatha.*
7. *Sañña.*
8. "Standard" is a translation of *pamāya,* meaning "having measured" or "defined."

Chapter 13: The Greater Discourse of the Dead End

1. "Array" is a translation of *vyūha* (in compound words, *v* becomes *b* when preceded by an *a*). *Vyūha,* here translated as "dead end," could possibly be read as the nominal form of *vyāharati,* meaning "to talk" or "to speak." The title of the *sutta* would then be the "Discourse on the Great Talk."
2. "Opinion" is a translation of *sammuti,* which could also be translated as "convention." *Puthujja* is translated by its common meaning of "separate" or "individual." *Puthujja* can also mean "commonplace" or "ordinary." But in the context of this *sutta's* emphasis on not getting involved in any doctrines, it seems more appropriate to translate it here using the broader term to render "any particular opinion" rather than "any common opinion."
3. "Go along with" is a translation of *khantimakubbamāno. Khantiṃ* means "patience," "acceptance"; *akubbamāno* means "not to do." *Khantiṃ* may be a scribal error for *kantiṃ,* meaning "desire," "love," or "be pleased." *Kantiṃ* is a variant reading in

some Pali editions; it is also how this word appears in the quotation of this verse in the Sanskrit text, the *Bodhisattva-bhūmi*.

4. The meaning of this sentence is obscure. To translate this line, most scholars look to the canonical commentary on this verse found in the *Niddesa* and borrow the idea that purity comes from self-restraint. I have tried to understand the sentence on its own terms, without the commentary. No English translation that I know of, including mine, translates *sañña* ("concept," "perception") in the opening phrase *sīluttamā saññamenāhu suddhiṃ*.
5. For the sake of clarity, I have translated *satthā* (caravan) as "traveler."
6. "Taking up peace" is a translation of *santi* (peace) + *anuggahāya. Anuggahāya* has two meanings. It is not clear which meaning applies or whether a conscious wordplay is intended here. Surprisingly, the word can mean either "not taking up" or "taking up." With the latter, it also means "assistance," "helping," and "having compassion for." Some translators have rendered the last phrase as "fostering peace." "Not taking up" seems the appropriate translation in the context of the emphasis on letting go found throughout the *Book of Eights*. To hold on to peace is not to have peace.
7. "Truth" is a translation of *tatha,* which can also mean "real."
8. "Words" is a translation of *saṅkhā,* which can mean a "definition," "word," "concept," or "name." In translating it as "words," I do so with reference to how it is used in "The Discourse on the Pathways of Names" (*Niruttipattha Sutta*), where it clearly means "word," "term," "name," or "designation" (*Saṃyutta Nikāya* 22.62; iii 71).

9. "Contaminants" is a translation of *āsava.*
10. The use of three words, each of which has two opposing meanings, may be wordplay here. The phrase could also be translated, "Being improper, not stopped, and not worth wanting."
11. "Laid their burden down" is a translation of *pannabhāro.* While this poem does not explain what the burden is, elsewhere in the *suttas,* it is said to be the conceit "I am" (*Middle Length Discourses* 22 at i 139). The word *pannabhāro* occurs thirteen times in the Pali discourses, mostly in poems that resemble the teachings in the *Book of Eights* (such as *Middle Length Discourses* 98, and *Numerical Discourses* 3.57, 5.179).

Chapter 14: The Discourse on Being Quick

1. "Freed" is a translation of *nibbāti.*
2. "Conceptual" is a translation of *saṅkhāya,* while "differentiation" is a translation of *papañca.*
3. "Release" is a translation of *nibbuti.*
4. Literally, "touched by many forms" (*rupa*).
5. "Embraced" and "rejected" are translations of *attā* and *nirattā,* respectively. *Attā* is taken here to be the past participle of *ādiyati,* "to take up, receive, or grasp." It is possible the word should be translated as "self," another meaning of *atta.* A wordplay may be intended.
6. "Discipline" is the translation of *pātimokkha,* the word for the code of monastic discipline. "Meditation" here is the translation of *samādhi,* a word usually translated as "concentration."
7. "Touched by sense experience" (*phassena yada phutthassa*) literally should be "touched by contact."
8. The list also includes "eatables" (*khaandiiya*). Since

this word is redundant with "food," I have omitted it. I believe it was included in the list for the sake of the poetic rhythm of the line.

9. *Āthabbanam* (Vedic spells and magic) refers to the *Artharva Veda,* a manual of mantras and magic rituals for healing, warfare, enemies, and significant rites of passage. It is one of the four most sacred Vedic texts.
10. The last two verses refer to the Buddha in the third person. They also refer to the Buddha with similar honorific titles as the questioner does in the opening verse. For these two reasons, I suggest that the last two verses belong to the questioner who provides concluding words instructing monastics to follow the instructions the Buddha has just given. In a communal recitation, the first verse and the last two may have been spoken by a lead chanter, with the Buddha's instruction chanted in unison by a group of monastics.
11. *Nibbuti.*

Chapter 15: The Discourse on Being Violent

1. "Being violent" is a loose translation of *atta* ("to take up or seize") and *daṇḍa* (meaning "stick" but often referring specifically to a rod used for punishment or as a weapon; by extension, the word sometimes refers to violence).
2. "Distress" or "dismay" is the translation of *saṃvega,* an important Buddhist concept. It is often thought of as a deep emotional agitation that arises when seeing the magnitude of suffering in the world. While it is hard to know more precisely what this emotion is, the Buddha

most commonly refers to it as a useful and appropriate emotion.

3. "Shaken" is the translation of *saṃvijitaṃ,* which can mean (1) "filled with fear" or "made to tremble," or (2) "felt" or "realized."
4. A more literal translation of "Everywhere things are changing" is "All directions are in motion" (*disā sabbā sameritā*).
5. This statement in the Pali text suggests that this discourse had, at one time, a liturgical role. Perhaps one person would recite the first part of the discourse and then the rest of the monastic community would recite the remaining part together.
6. "Full release" is a translation of *nibbāna.*
7. "Violent" is a translation of *sāhasā,* which can also mean "rash, hasty, or arbitrary action."
8. "Attractive" is a translation of *Ākāsa,* which also can mean (empty) "space."
9. The first three lines of this verse also appear in Dhammapada verse 367.
10. This might also be translated as "Or [concerned] that things [belong] to others" (*paresaṃ vāpi kiñcanaṃ*).
11. The commentaries explain "accumulation" (*nisaṅkhati*) as referring to the accumulation of merit and demerit as well as of karma.

Chapter 16: The Discourse to Sāriputta

1. Verses 955–62 are in the *śloka* meter (four lines with eight syllables each), while verses 963–75 are in the *triṣṭubh* meter (four lines with eleven syllables each).
2. "Who is Thus" is a translation of *tādiṃ.* Literally this word means "such" or "such like." In context it can

mean "of such [good qualities]." I have chosen the literal meaning as it fits the title the Buddha often called himself, Tathāgata, meaning "The One Who is Thus." The word is also used in verse 803.

3. It is hard to know how to translate *vijigucchato,* rendered here as "disaffected." The *Pali-English Dictionary* suggests the word means "to loathe." It seems the commentary explains it as meaning "worried." Norman translates it as "disgusted," and Saddhatissa as "abhors the world."
4. "Going where never gone before" refers to nirvana.
5. "Solitary" is a translation of *ekodi.* The word can also mean "unified" when it is used in describing meditation states. Because the *Book of Eights* doesn't discuss the details of meditation, and because the rest of this *sutta* emphasizes living in secluded places, I have chosen to translate it as "solitary."
6. Verse 239 of the Dhammapada could be the reply to the question of this verse. The last two lines of both verses are the same.
7. "Living restrained" is a translation of *sapariyantacārī*; *sa* = with; *pariyanta* = limits or restrictions; *cārī* = one who lives or behaves.
8. "Contact" is a translation of *phassa,* which commonly refers to sense contact or touch. Occasionally, as an adjective, it can mean "pleasing or beautiful sensations."
9. "Firm in their exertion" is a translation of *parakkammadaḷham.* I am unsure how to understand *parakkamma. Para* can mean "other" as well as "other shore." Can *parakkamma* mean "service to others"?
10. "Should live" is a translation of *tiṭṭhe,* which more

literally means "should stand." Other translators have translated it as "stand firm."

11. "Masters" is a translation of *addhābhavanto.*
12. "Admirable" is a translation of *kalyāṇa.*
13. "Agitated" is a translation of *pādalolo* (*pāda* = "foot"; *lola* = "agitated, wavering").
14. "Practicing meditation" is a translation of *jhānānuyutto* (*jhāna* = "meditation"; *anuyutto* = "engaged with, practicing").
15. "Surliness" is a translation of *khila,* which refers to wasteland or fallow land, and figuratively the word is used to refer to a barren or obstructed mind. I believe *khila* here is meant to be an opposite reaction to being happy when reprimanded.
16. Here I am taking *sahetha* as coming from *sahati* ("to conquer"). I wonder if *sahetha* comes from *sahetu,* in which case, this sentence should be, "They should train to remove the five stains of the world, [namely] the stains caused by forms, sounds, tastes, smells, and touch." "Passion" is a translation of *rāga.*
17. "Perfect" is a translation of *sammā,* a word most commonly translated into English as "right" or "proper."
18. "Concentrated" is a translation of *ekodi.*

Afterword

1. K. R. Norman suggests that because none of the individual *suttas* from the *Book of Eights* is quoted in full in the rest of the Pali canon, the anthology was seen as "original and indivisible" from "the very earliest period of Buddhism"; see Norman, *The Group of*

Discourses (Oxford: Pali Text Society, 2001), xxxvi. He supports this idea by pointing out that the early commentary, the *Niddesa,* treats the *Book of Eights* as an independent, complete work (xxxi). See also Oskar Von Hinüber, *A Handbook of Pāli Literature* (Berlin: Walter de Gruyer, 1996), 49–50.

2. Norman, *Group of Discourses,* xxxi.
3. Von Hinüber, *Handbook,* 99.
4. The *Book of Eights* is mentioned in *Hāliddakāni Sutta* 1 (*Saṃyutta Nikāya* 22.3). A second mention is found in the *Soṇa Sutta* (*Udana* 5.6). The story in the *Soṇa Sutta,* as well as its mention of the *Book of Eights,* is also found in the *Vinaya* I 196. The *Book of the Way to the Other Shore* is mentioned at *Saṃyutta Nikāya* 12.31 and at *Aṅguttara Nikāya* 3.32, 3.33, 4.41, 6.61, and 7.53.
5. Norman, *Group of Discourses,* xxxiii–xxxiv.
6. Erich Frauwallner (*The Earliest Vinaya and the Beginnings of Buddhist Literature* [Rome: Instituto Italiano Per Il Medio Ed Estremo Oriente, 1956], 149) mentions that the story of Soṇa reciting the *Book of Eights* occurs in the surviving *Vinaya* from all the early Buddhist schools.
7. The *Yizu Jing* (T 198) translated by Zhi Qian. For an English translation of this Chinese text, see P. V. Bapat, *Arthapada Sutra: Spoken by the Buddha.* Visva-Bharati Studies 13, 1951.
8. Norman, *Group of Discourses,* xxxix.
9. *Saṃyutta Nikāya* 22.3.
10. *Udana* 5.6 and *Vinaya* I 196.
11. *Aṅguttara Nikāya* 2.37; I 66.
12. *Middle Length Discourses* 18.
13. *Middle Length Discourses* 133.

14. The Buddha recites verse 842 from "The Discourse to Māgaṇḍiya" in the *Samiddhi Sutta* in the *Saṃyutta Nikāya* 1.20 (i 12).

Select Bibliography

Translations

Bagchi, Prabodh Chandra. "The Arthapada-Sūtra Spoken by the Buddha," in *Visva-Bharati Annals,* vol. 1, 1945 (135–227), and vol. 3, 1950 (1–109). (English translation of the Chinese version of the *Book of Eights.*)

Fausböll, V. *The Sutta Nipāta: A Collection of Discourses.* Sacred Books of the East, vol. 10, pt. 2. Oxford: Clarendon Press, 1881.

Hare, E. M. *Woven Cadences of Early Buddhists* (*Sutta-Nipāta*). London: Oxford University Press, 1945.

Ireland, John. *The Discourse Collection: Selected Texts from the Sutta Nipata.* Wheel Publication no. 82. Kandy, Sri Lanka: Buddhist Publication Society, 1965.

Norman, K. R. *The Group of Discourses.* Oxford: Pali Text Society, 2001.

Saddhatissa, Hammalawa. *The Sutta-Nipāta*. London: Curzon Press, 1985.

Thanissaro, Bhikkhu. "The Atthaka Vagga: The Octet Chapter" (Metta Forest Monastery, 1997), http://www.accesstoinsight.org/lib/authors/thanissaro/atthakavagga.html.